By Nolan Recker

Copyright © 2015 by Nolan Ryan Recker
All rights reserved. This book or any portion thereof
may not be reproduced or used in any manner whatsoever
without the express written permission of the publisher
except for the use of brief quotations in a book review.

Printed in the United States of America

Edited by Katie Clayton

Unless otherwise cited, all of the Bible quotations are from the Holman Christian Standard Bible.

Table of Contents

Dear Reader	4
0: Beginnings	5
1: Through A Painted Question	18
2: O.M.G.	23
3: Transparency & A Weak Literary Transition	40
4: Starting Points	44
5: Well This is Awkward	54
6: Tom Sawyer & Huck Finn Theology	64
7: The Good, Bad, and Charlton Heston, Again?	69
8: Jesus Superstar!	81
9: Faith, Simply	90
10: Love Bug, It Stinks! Wait, It's A Stink Bug!	101
11: Are You Allowed To Talk About Sex In A Christian Book?	109
Parting Thoughts	122

Dear Reader,

Thank you for taking the time to make it past the front cover.

Regarding the title, it is the same title of a song recorded during a worship gathering in 2003 by Jason Upton and his band.

In the song it is said, "I declare over you, God has given you the air…"

to pursue "new perspectives…"

an "aerial view…"

Rise up and consider God from a new perspective and

fly.

Chapter 0:
Beginnings

At what point did we begin?

This is an abstract question, but trek with me.

At what point did I commence living?

When did I *start*?

Did my life start at conception?

How about my first birthday?

Did it begin the first time I thought I was going to die?

Or,

did it begin when my parents started thinking about having a child?

My wife and I had our first child in June of 2015. Before finding out we were pregnant, we talked about the idea of a boy or a girl. We asked various questions and discussed different scenarios.

Part of those conversations asked the question,

"What is our baby going to be like?"

There were late night musings about what features our child would have. We described in detail the ideal traits he or she would inherit from us. We created what we thought to be a picturesque version of our child. These conversations inspired the thinking of *beginning*.

About three months into the pregnancy, we were able to find out the gender of our child. We were excited to learn we would have a boy!

To say I was stoked, excited, flabbergasted, emotional, unaware, expectant, strategizing, praying, reading, learning, talking, thinking, listening, more praying, ostentatious, giddy, confused, ignorant, doubtful, hopeful, open-minded, with an overall sense of "Hey, we are having a kid!"

would have been an understatement.

To be honest, we were not planning on having a child for another year or so. In the very least we planned on *trying* to have a child sometime in 2016. I guess that is how it goes with planning. However, we like how it turned out. There was not an expectation of when it would happen, so it eliminated the potential for disappointment.

Crazy.

It is all part of the birthing process. Creating a new thing.

Which brings me back to my thought on *beginning…*

When did our child first come to life?

Was it when we first found out we were pregnant?

Was it when we found out it was a boy?

Was it when we determined his name?

Maybe it was the moment I first felt him kick. It definitely set in with the increased frequency of my wife's change in tastes and late night trips to the gas station for a slushy.

For me, our child first *came alive* long before we were pregnant.

Before finding out we were having a boy, we would talk about what it would be like to have a child of either gender.

If our baby were a girl then I know I would spoil the mess out of her and we would have been best friends. I would avoid the *becoming a woman talk* with her and would have left that to her mother.

Ew.

I looked forward to meeting our son. So far, I am learning a lot about what it means to be a *father* and train him to become a better man than me. I look forward to the chats discussing how men are to receive and practice love, give and earn respect, and partner with God.

Our son has been alive to us for quite some time. But, when will *he* first feel alive?

When will his *journey* begin?

Psalm 84:5 says "Happy are the people whose strength is in [The Lord], whose hearts are set on pilgrimage."

One way to define pilgrimage is: *a long journey, maybe even a quest.*

When does his journey begin? He's only a baby. What quest does he have to take?

For our parents, their journey of us began long before our earliest memory. I do not remember my journey up the proverbial canal racing past other versions of myself on a quest to the promised land.

Do you?

As I journeyed my way into the cold abyss, how much do I remember from my quest as I reached toward the light for the first time, screaming because I just wanted to get pushed back in?

None.

Did my journey in life begin when I felt the warm embrace of my mother?

Maybe it was the first time I slept and awoke feeling refreshed, or hungry. Probably hungry. Actually, I am hungry now.

Maybe it was the first time I remember feeling pain?

Maybe our journey begins whenever we realize our life is a gift, an opportunity we might not have had if it were not for the journeys of the people who made you.

I believe *life*,

regardless of creed or belief, is something given.

A gift.

I think we can agree as infants we probably wanted to live. It is intrinsic in our DNA to stay alive.

As infants we may not have had the consciousness to possess an existential thought or feeling about life, but there is something that was woven into our subconscious to love life!

Sure, my son gets fussy whenever he is hungry or tired, but all he is trying to convey is,

I need to be replenished,

I need to be refreshed.

For many of us, this journey we call life is something we cherish. We grew up in a home where our basic needs were met. Our parents gave us a chance to succeed.

For others, life was not this way. It is a burden.

You were a burden. In your mind you may have wondered, *why am I even here?*

From the moment your mother found out she was pregnant until the day you hopelessly pass, your mother and probably absent father never matured and became the people you needed them to be.

We either celebrate life or we condemn it. Criticize it. Or could care less about it.

Celebration is a choice.

Condemnation, criticism, and apathy require little effort.

How we see and understand *life*, matters.

Our *perspective* matters.

Perspective drives how we *think and perceive.*

Here is an example:

After high school and into my graduate school years, I would go back to the elementary school and visit the remaining faculty members leftover from years I attended the school.

I made sure to inform my teachers I was attending a Christian College and was still a Christian.

After I graduated college, I made sure to return and encourage them, "Hey! I graduated college! Thank you for all you did for me when I was a student here."

After graduate school I went back one last time. There were only a few people left who recognized me. One of which was my teacher from Kindergarten, Miss Brackman. She was the only teacher who was present for all of my visits.

On this final trip all the Kindergarten kids asked, "who are you?"

Miss Brackman and I attempted to explain how I was once their age. I said, "Miss Brackman was my Kindergarten teacher! A long time ago!"

One child's mouth dropped open as their eyes doubled in size.

Another scoffed at the idea, "No way!"

Another child poked me and walked away unimpressed.

A couple children looked at me, back at Miss Brackman, back at me, pursed their bottom lips and slightly nodded their heads as if they were thinking, "O.K. I don't get it, but O.K."

One straight up said, "You're crazy!" and then proceeded to go back to gluing something.

I had the thought, I used to be one of those kids!

What a perspective shift. Then I thought through each year I attended the school.

From Kindergarten until graduation as I became one of the "big kids," the size of the school building shrank.

As I got bigger,
the school got smaller.

Even when additions were made to the school and it expanded, it still seemed to shrink. Whenever I visited I tried to imagine how big it all felt when I attended there.

As a student I formed a *mindset* about the school. As my perspective changed it challenged my mindset. In an attempt to understand the school differently, I tried to alter my mindset by considering a new perspective.

This brings me back to our life-journey. What is your current mindset and perspective influencing that mindset?

I submit for your consideration that what gives way to the importance of our *mindset* and our life as a *journey* is a perspective that all life has *purpose*.

My lungs expand with oxygen and give life to the blood and my heart pumps the blood and gives life to my body.

I wake up in the morning and determine what I want to accomplish that day and then proceed to do it.

There is a difference between my internal muscles and my mindset.

Although my muscles do not have a choice, they do have a purpose. Their purpose is to give my body the means to life. They are not open to considering their *purpose for being* or hearing another person's *opinion* about their purpose. They do what they can do until they are no longer able to do it.

My mindset is consistently questioned by my thoughts and the thoughts of others. With so much information out there and the access to said information, I have found it difficult to determine where to begin.

I ask myself the question,

What gives *purpose* to my life?

I guess it is a matter of perspective. Some would say I need to live *for* something.

What if I live for me?
What if I became the wealthiest person ever?
What if I want more wives and concubines than King Solomon?
What if I pursued a legacy? That people would always remember the name,

Nolan Recker.

What if I build the largest non-profit organization benefiting millions of people?

What if I become a hard-core religious freak?

The list could go on…

Maybe my life-journey begins whenever I discover my *purpose.*

It gives an intended destination to my quest.

Consider the following pages as a signpost on the road of your journey.

What is your mindset about the things of God?

Simply put, I think the things of God—mainly, how he see us and how we see him—matter in every person's journey.

Too many of us try to oversimplify God and then wonder why we have a hard time reconciling many of what we think are contradictions about God compared to what we believe about him.

At this point in my journey, I have been a Christian for the better part of twenty-one years. I am close to turning thirty.

Yikes.

Believing in God for over two-thirds of my life has directly influenced my mindset and how I perceive the world.

My perspective is always changing. Partly because I choose to alter my perspective and partly because things happen causing a necessary shift in perspective.

At times, I feel like Nicodemus. You can read about him in John 3. He beheld a certain mindset his entire life until Jesus came along and said, "Be born again."

Nico asked how was a man to go back into his mother in order to be *born again*.

Jesus then went on to explain how he must use earthly parallels to describe the Kingdom of Heaven. In order to understand spiritual truths, we have to be born again.

It is improbable to see heaven with an earthly perspective.

It is impossible for us to understand heaven with an earthly mindset.

Our old mindset must be exchanged for a new one. We have to have a new beginning.

It was about four years ago something clicked in my spirit awakening me to the presence of God. Because of this, it feels like my relationship with God has accelerated. It feels like I am learning more than what I am able to retain, but maybe it is supposed to feel this way. Just when I feel I can catch up, God is moving on to the next thing.

That's the journey of it, though. Life has its ups and downs. However, the ups and downs, the ebb and flow, make more sense when encountered with a sense purpose.

It came to life for me in an unreal way around the time I turned twenty-five.

God is one of many explanations for *purpose*.

I believe, God purposed something in me those four years ago when God's *grace* awakened in me. I wrote this book not to change your mindset, but to offer a different perspective.

It was not until the last visit at my elementary school when I stopped and stared at my surroundings and realized,

I had grown.

By grown, I mean more than physically.

My understanding had grown. Each visit painted a more detailed portrait of the distance between that place and the person who stood covered in nostalgia.

Spiritually, I had been formed. Along the way, something was birthed within me that did not require me returning to attend elementary school to learn it all over again.

However, the more I *grew* the more God *shrank*.

In my years of growth, it felt like I experienced more hurdles to my faith than actual encounters with God.

Standing and staring at the school, I was no longer the oldest of five children who witnessed two divorces; the second of which was filled with domestic abuse and a step-father addicted to cocaine. The same kid who was a charity case and probably one of the poorer kids in the joint. I faired well academically. I was an above average basketball player who set a couple records. It was during my sixth grade year when I set those records and also settled on forgetting God and never looking back.

At that time I had the sense of, "Thanks for a whole lot of nothing, "God."

The God I knew was of little interest to me.

If it was not for the father of a friend of mine—whom was the coach for our twelve year-old fall baseball team— whom reached out to a hurting kid, I would have gotten lost for awhile. I was ready to lash out for attention and all that. What they did was help me see God in a different way. They helped me see God from a different perspective.

Altering my perspective helped shift my perception and birth a new mindset within me. They helped me see there were many decent people in the world. It gave me hope for a God whom seemed distant and cold.

The God I knew was a God you did your best to keep happy. The Bible said he loved the world and sent Jesus, but if you screwed up just one time then you would go to hell or something terrible like Azkaban.

My understanding was, "Fear not! For God is merciful. So just humble yourself, be impoverished, and serve everyone and then maybe God will let you into heaven. Good luck."

Most of my life consisted of trying to make God happy. It was all about what I did.

Not many people spoke of God's kindness. They spoke about his hatred of evil.

They also said I am an evil person and do not deserve heaven, but if I were to trust in this Jesus fellow then he will save me from God. Technically, they are the same, but we have a hard time explaining it, so to simplify:

God was, and kind of is, still pissed about the whole sin thing, but believe that Jesus died for your sins, ask him into your heart and you will have salvation! "Trust us, you want salvation, it means going to heaven. Yay!"

Man could God hold a grudge! Even though Jesus had died almost 2,000 years before I was born, God was already mad about my sins and required Jesus, straight away, for the remission of my sins.

My mindset needed to be born again, exchanged for another one.

Our perspective and perception can also be defined as a *worldview*. It is the way we see the world. Our experiences and indoctrinations drive our worldview.

Worldview is an action.

Mindset is a state.

Shifting our worldview allows for the birthing or *transformation* of our mindset.

Transformation can happen *to us* or we can partner in bringing it about *in us*. It kind of depends on our thoughts concerning the transition.

The chapters in this book are some things of God I did not understand in part at the ages of twelve, eighteen, or twenty-one. Most of this stuff I did not begin to learn until I was twenty-five. The way in which I have come to understand the topics in the following chapters has been revolutionary in my relationship with God.

Anything before this time seemed like a continual desert of unanswered questions and perpetuated doubt. Not a single drop of rain to wet my lips. Just empty ideas and glimpses of what may or may not have been God.

I have experienced a transformed mindset in all of the following topics. Perpetual questions met with revelatory answers and a greater appreciation for whom I believe to be the creator of all good things.

The Bible talks about a guy named Moses. He was a man who knew God's ways, yet the people that Moses led only knew what God had done.

The people focused on the *product* while Moses participated in the *process*.

The purpose of me writing this book is to participate in a well-intentioned conversation concerning not just the *things* of God, but to encourage every reader in their journey to know the *ways* of God.

For as far as Christianity is concerned, our battle in this life is not between the righteous man and the sinner, the saved and the lost, but against something that is within all of us.

> "For although we are walking in the flesh [according to what we can see], we do not wage war in a fleshly way, since the weapons of our warfare are not fleshly [tangible objects that can be held], but are powerful through God for the demolition of strongholds. We demolish arguments and every high-minded thing that is raised up against the knowledge of God, taking every thought captive to the obedience of Christ [reminding ourselves of Christ Jesus' obedience and not our obedience to Him]." 2 Corinthians 10:3-5 Brackets are mine.

Maybe ask yourself,

What are the things influencing how I see the world?

How does God see me?

What is his mindset about me?

How do I see God?

What is my mindset?

What is my purpose?

What are the hurdles in your relationship to God?

I hope we can all grow through what I have written here. In addition to praying to God, we read and study in an effort to grow and mature in our relationship with him.

As we move into the next chapter, keep the following quote in the back of your mind.

N.T. Wright said,

"The reason why it is important to study worldviews is that human life is complicated, confusingly multifaceted, and often puzzling…

"[We must] move from the one-dimensional world of disembodied ideas to the three-dimensional world of ordinary, full human life,

"the initial confusion caused by all the new elements will be rewarded, one may hope, by clarity, nuance, perspective and even, perhaps relevance."

"A great deal of what humans do, say and think appears to spring from deep buried sources…

"It is better to recognize this, and to make continual attempts to map the resulting mystery, "rather than to imagine that all of life can be understood in the flat, obvious surface events, statements and apparent meaning.

"The seemingly disparate elements of human life join up in ways which are easy to experience but hard to describe,

"but which are perceived to be very important;

"hence, for a start, the irreducibly and appropriate metaphorical nature of all human discourse, and the cultural importance of novels, plays and the cinema."

We are pursuing a like-minded understanding of things related to God as presented through stories, study, experience, and meanderings.

To bring together what, at first glance seems to be inconsistent perspectives and perceptions into a transformed mindset to further you on your life-journey with God.

Let's start the conversation.

Chapter 1:
Through a Painted Question

There is this painting hanging in our home.

My wife's grandmother painted it.

It is a beach setting with two sand dunes. Near the bottom of the painting there are little marks in the sand indicative of footprints. They lead from the left moving right toward the smaller dune where they stop. I think the painting is peaceful. It stirs up memories in me. There is one particular memory I would like to share with you.

My wife and I got married in a small church with a pastor friend and two witnesses to boot. It was the end of the tax year and we planned to jointly file our taxes in the spring. A wam-bam-thank-you-mam ceremony that lasted all but five minutes and culminated with a late night trip to Steak-N-Shake to celebrate the occasion.

No dress.

No tux.

No flowers.
We donned hooded sweatshirts, jeans, jackets, and hearts full of hope and love. I guess some of us had shirts, underwear, socks, and shoes too, but the devil is in the details.

Before the ceremony, we toyed with the idea of doing something small, but never settled on it. We knew the grand sha-bang of weddings was not going to happen for a time. It came down to a chilly day in December. After we spoke with financially inclined people and with her parents, we decided to tie the knot.

We got hitched.

A covenant was formed.

Fast forward five months and hours of planning, we set off for the Outer Banks of North Carolina to do what every little girl dreams of doing.

We gathered together.

We dressed to the nines.

We had ourselves a party to celebrate all parties. The joining of two people into one covenant.

Our family and friends joined us too.

It was amazing.
My wife with her father walked together down a small dune with maybe twenty other people looking on. Dressed in white, stunning, tear-jerkingly stunning. Sorry, give me a moment.

With each step her smile grew wider. My father-in-law's ability to fight back tears grew weaker. My eyes without fail—I love weddings—welled up with joy as I watched my bride make her way toward me, to stand in the moment,

with me.

For me.

From my perspective, I was about to receive the greatest prize this side of heaven.

I waited as my father-in-law hugged and kissed his daughter. She left his embrace and joined me toe to toe, hand in hand. Two people entered into a moment where they were reminded of the purposeful intentionality they vowed to practice for the rest of their days.

The painting our grandmother gifted to us captured the scene.

When we first unwrapped the painting an ocean of emotions welled up inside of us as we realized the setting, "this is where we got married!"

I know we had the small ceremony five months earlier, but there is something special when we celebrate the joy and opportunity of marriage between two people. We stood surrounded by our closest family and friends, as we intend to do for the rest of our days.

The footprints in the painting are the same path Emma and her father took to meet me in front of the small sandy bump with the rough straw and combed over grass. I relive those moments in detail whenever I soak in the rich history of the painted tapestry.

It is different than a photograph, ya know? Photographs are fantastic, instantly igniting the same sentiment felt within your mind and heart on that day. However, paintings require a different type of appreciation.

Like any solid marriage, it takes time to really get the hang of it.

It is true, some photographs took hours of preparation and waiting to capture the ideal moment. However, paintings are in a league of their own.

It is an investment, every careful stroke made with purpose. Layer by layer, brush stroke by brush stroke, the masterpiece takes shape. Like paintings, the appreciation I had at first for my wife will mature and grow as I reach completion.

In a way, our grandmother began the process for us in the way of a painting. Every time we look at it we remember the moment she captures so well on canvas. We hope the painting and the story lasts for generations.

Imagine our excitement then as we realized the painting's significance. Of course, we had to share this with everyone. We took a picture of it and posted it online for others to sing its praises. Outwardly we adorned our grandmother with thanksgiving as she gave us a unique gift.

What we did not know at the time of our initial excitement was the *other* story behind the painting.

It had been a couple weeks in between the seaside ceremony and the celebratory gathering we held in Illinois. We wanted to celebrate and have a reason to gather together with other friends and family who were unable to make the trip to the coast. This was the day we received many gifts and the beloved painting. That night, we ripped off the wrapping paper from around the painting. We let gratitude crash over us thinking grandma had painted it during the two weeks we returned from North Carolina.

Seems logical.

It was not for another week or so after the reception we got to have lunch with grandma. Of course, we thanked her. We said something along the lines of "Thank you so much! We appreciate you taking the time to paint the scene of where we got married!"

She replied, "Oh yeah, I am glad you like it. I was going to give you another painting of a boat, but then I kept looking and found that one."

Wait…

Found?

She continued, "Oh yeah! I painted that, probably over twenty-five years ago! She (pointing to my mother-in-law) was not even pregnant with Emma, yet."

Coincidence? Maybe…

We picked our jaws up off the floor. Then Emma and I looked at each other and back at grandma, "You painted that before Emma was, well, wait, what?"

"Oh yeah." She said that a lot. "It just goes to show that God had this planned all along."

Emma and I were speechless.

See, I had been married before I met Emma. Tragically, it came to an end for reasons outside of my control, but God did not pre-ordain the divorce of my first marriage. However, God's grace went before, during, and after that marriage. He redeemed both my story and Emma's.

I imagine the whole restaurant dropped eaves on our conversation and joined us in picking our jaws up off the floor. My wife's grandmother painted the detailed scene where Emma would get handed off by her father to be married.

More so, we planned on using a different spot for the ceremony. At the last minute we decided to change locations. Beyond that, grandma had never been to the Outer Banks in her life. No joke. I could make up this stuff, but the reality is far too exciting.

I mean, it could be something you find in a Nicholas Sparks book. The dude can write some love stories. If you didn't know, many of his stories take place in the Carolinas. He is from there. If you have never been there, put this book down and plan your trip. You will not regret it. And if you have not heard of Sparks, read *The Notebook*.

Or watch the movie because that Ryan Gosling is a dream. And Rachel McAdams? Don't make me blush.

I am not sure what this narrative meant to our grandmother, but she was convinced God knew Emma and I were gonna get together. For some, they would exclaim, "Amen! Preach!" However, for others, the response may not be as quick to affirm such a perspective.

My perspective on the painting and the ways of God was worth something. It had to be more than a *coincidence*. It begged the question,

what do I believe about God?

I appreciate the thought of Donald Miller regarding beliefs for or against an almighty deity:

"I felt as if believing in God was no more rational than having an imaginary friend. They have names for people who have imaginary friends, you know. They keep them in special hospitals. Maybe my faith in God was a form of insanity. Maybe I was losing my marbles. I start believing in Christ, and the next thing you know I am having tea with the Easter Bunny or waltzing with my toaster, shouting, "The redcoats are coming!""

Reading those words compared to words of a similar subject matter written by Donald tens years later would offer a different perspective. That is the thing about perspective, circumstances change or transform the way we see things.

If your idea of God is negative, then I hope my perspective will help with seeing a positive side of God. If your idea of God is positive, but has plateaued or gotten stuck, then my hope is to dislodge you from your position long enough to uncover something new about God.

Chapter 2:
O.M.G. (Oh my God)

A good starting place in answering the question of *what do I believe about God*, is to answer this question:

Who is God?

That was the question I had to answer for an assignment in college. The class was called Essentials of Theology.

My thesis for the paper was "God is..."

Consider me a man of many words.

Inevitably, my thesis also became my conclusion. I concluded even with Scripture's immense amount of descriptions and names for God, the best description I had for God was, *God is*.

That's it. Real helpful, right?

Pastor Judah Smith recently published a book titled *Jesus is, _____*. Judah fills in the blank with different adjectives, verbs, and nouns to describe Jesus. His book is a lot better than my paper from college. I should have added a line!
The purpose of the assignment was to answer the question Judah laid out in his book.

Who is *God*?

Or,

Whom is God?

Grab your head before it starts to spin. I received a failing grade on my paper. The professor, whom I had and still have immense respect for and learned a lot from, described my idea as "creative," but I missed the point of the assignment. There are plenty of things in the Bible useful in describing the personhood and character of God.

He said if I were to add some of those Scripture-founded definitions for God, my grade could be reworked and I would not have to settle for a failing mark. I took advantage of the opportunity because back then it was not worth the fight. Christianity is all about *humility* after all. Also, I was not in a position to change his mind. My attempt to dislodge his perspective, appeared to have failed.

Essentials of Theology discussed the essentials of studying God. It flew in the face of anything I previously understood. I was a twenty-one year old male with a brain that was not yet fully developed— specifically the prefrontal cortex— attending a Bible College. My brain still had years of development left before allowing me the opportunity to fully consider future consequences of present decisions.

I was young and impressionable, but I sought to be a free thinker. The God I knew was big enough to allow for me to truly seek His heart, who He was and is; free to make mistakes without having to worry about offending Him.

God is a pretty *stand-up* God. Anyone I have ever met who could be considered a honorable or stand-up individual is not easily, if ever, offended by the ignorance of another person. This concept is easier to accept whenever we consider the innocence of the person. For example, it is one thing when a child walks up to a woman with a slightly rounded belly, pokes it and with their cute bubbly eyes says, "Baby?"

Now, it is easier to forgive a child, but what about an adult? If I were to walk up to a stranger, poke her in the belly and say, "Baby?" The embarrassment and frustration may be elevated because I am adult, and "Adults don't ask bigger women if they are pregnant!"

For a short time after college and returning to Lincoln for graduate school, I lived in my uncle's pool hut in the backyard. Living with either of my parents was not an option so I bounced around. There were a few benefits to living in that hut. It was a little bigger than what you may imagine a *hut* to be and so track with me here. There was a futon for sitting and sleeping. There was a mini fridge, and it also had a sturdy roof.

Other than those amenities, it was completely open to the elements, lacking enclosed windows or a door.

One Saturday, my cousins came out of the house to play in the pool. I did not have to work, so I swam and hung out on the deck with them. While relaxing on the pool deck my four-year-old cousin walked up to me and poked me in the nipple.

Yup.

Straight shot.

As she poked my nipple she said, "Boob!"

I laughed and corrected her, "No, that is a nipple."

She poked it again and affirmed, "Boob!"

After correcting her again, she insisted and poked again. I laughed. A lot. It is easy to not be offended when I do not have to worry about the offender or the subject.

I think a healthy way to live is to have a certain openness to change one's mind about certain things. The Bible uses the word, *repent.*

This was the whole basis for John the Baptist's ministry. Beginning with him and continuing into the 21st century, the Kingdom of God collides with world-focused perception. "The time is fulfilled, and the kingdom of God has come near. Repent and believe in the good news!"

That word, *repent.*

Your current perspective will render a positive or negative response. Maybe you rendered an indifferent response. Fair enough. For some, that word leaves an icky taste in their mouth.

Many evangelical Christians use it as the go to word for exposing sin and threatening damnation by hellfire: A sulfuric lake of said hellfire.

Yum.

Moy caliente.

Never mind, gross. Sulfur wreaks of rotten eggs. I digress.

Have you seen the signs worn by those "called by God" to stand there and proclaim the end of the world? They may read something along the lines of,

"REPENT! FOR THE END IS NEAR."

"Repent or perish."

"Repent and turn from your sin."

"Repent or die."

A quick Google Image search for *repent* will give a glimpse of the gross mishandling and misunderstanding of this word.

The thing about *repent* is its roots, its origin dates back to Latin. Then it went to Old French and then Middle English before getting to what we have today! For your own curiosity, look up how many derivations of English exist.

What's the point?

Language is messy and should be handled appropriately. The way we describe God, matters.

We use the Bible as the foundation for describing God. There are assumed cautions with this approach. Translating ancient documents is a lengthy process. Things happen as the text is passed down from generation to generation. The struggle is keeping the historical context and the present-day interpretation connected.

Scholars and academics do their best to make modern translations as readable as possible. The New Testament was written in Koine Greek. The ancient writers used more words to describe similar things. In the English language we often use one word to describe many things. It is easier in print to differentiate between words, but phonetically, English becomes one of the most difficult languages to learn. For example, *there, their, and they're.* How about throwing a ball, a spherical object, or throwing a ball, going to a dance. Why would I throw a dance? That is silliness.

Furthermore, Koine Greek would slightly alter original words in order to better describe what it was they were trying to communicate. The Greeks did their best to create words by joining two or more words together in order to define people, places, and things.

Language is hard.

Back to *repent*.

Whenever we see *repent,* there is a variation of the same word behind it in Koine Greek. The noun is *metanoia*. The verbal cognate of the word is *metanoeo*. Surprisingly, this is not anything new. Many people have instituted in their corners of the Internet explanations clarifying how *repent* is a poor substitute for *metanoia*.

If this is new to you, then you are in for a treat. If this is not the first time you heard this then cheers to you. I hope you find some other morsels of depth to continue you on your journey. Let this serve as much needed encouragement in the battle for our minds and hearts.

The biggest battle we have to fight is not against flesh, sickness, death, the government (depends on who you ask), or other evil forces; but it is against the unseen, what the Apostle Paul describes in 2 Corinthians 10, mainly our held perceptions of God's love for us.

Metanoia means to <u>change one's thoughts about a given thing or idea.</u>

The Biblical context implies that people, particularly of the Ancient Jewish variety were under the strict impression the only way to have a blessed life was to please God by keeping his commandments. Unfortunately, up until Jesus, not a single person had been able to keep every command; and somehow not incur God's wrath by killing some animal (which had to be without any imperfection) to appease the Creator of the Universe. By that point in time people had become quite jaded, bitter, and fearful about the whole unable to please God, thing.

Thankfully, God knew from its induction, the Law and sacrificial system wasn't perfect, as the writer of Hebrews describes in chapter 10 of their book. God pre-determined the point in history when Jesus would walk the earth and redeem the people.

Before the cross, Jesus walked the earth to show exactly what God looked like, literally. It says in Psalms Moses knew God's *ways* and the Israelites knew his *acts.* The point is, because of the mass confusion about the heart of God, he became flesh in the embodiment of Jesus to walk out the exact affections of God for his creation. God revealing himself as Father through his Son. It was John the Baptist and Jesus (God in the flesh) who in so many words cried out,

"People! It's time to have a new thought about God! He is doing something *new*!"

I wonder what went through their minds. "I have heard this before. Some *savior* coming to tell us he has all of the answers, I'll believe it when I see it." The sad part is many saw the things that Jesus did and still did not believe Jesus was anything more than a nuisance.

When I was a smaller version of myself, aged maybe four or five years, I had an affinity for treasure hunting inside my nostrils. It is a disgusting habit for a child, especially one with an undocumented attention deficit hyperactive disorder or what we'll call a wild imagination.

My finger managed to find its way north and pick out a whole bunch of thing. It gives me the willies to think about it now, but back then I would let gravity take over after taking hold of the prize slipping from my nose toward my mouth.

Gag.

I did not know any better. Of course my parents did and they did their best to deter my behavior. What does bacteria and social order mean to a kindergartener?

I will tell you. It means

nothing.

This is because I did not understand what it meant to be embarrassed. *What you gonna do about that, Ma?* My mom's older sister and my much adored aunt would stick up for me. She would always see the oppositional and sometimes better sides of things. "Oh let him go, it's a good source of protein!" I love my aunt, but as Jimmy Fallon's alter ego Sara might say,

"Ew!"

I appreciated the support, I think, but still—gross.

At the time, I did not have a single thought on the subject. Some years down the road, I started a new habit. I broke the recreational booger picking and opted for a worse health risk. I chewed my nails.

I would go to town on those things. I think by that time I understood what it meant to be embarrassed, so I will chalk the habit up to stress. Well done, stress. You overcame a junior high boy late to the puberty party, I hope you're proud of yourself.

I chewed my nails for a few years.

I had plenty of people explain the disgusting facts surrounding the aforementioned habit. This time, I did not care to stop for reasons other than ignorance. It is not that I could not stop, there was something in me that did not want to stop. I was not hurting anyone, *what's the problem?*

It was not until the end of my eighth grade year something happened. Looking back, I do not know if I heard something about it or if I fabricated the illusion, but one day it all changed.

I *believed*,

if I continue to chew my nails in high school, I would not make any new friends.

I went to junior high at a small private school. There were nineteen kids in my graduating class. The public high school had over 1,300.

I did not want to be a loser.

Somehow, chewing nails and making friends correlated in some way. You can have one, but you cannot have both.

What did I do about it?

I stopped.

Just like that. One day I am chewing them, and the next day I am not chewing them. It has not changed. Not one desire to chew my nails. Same with eating nasal nuggets. Ew.

I repented of biting my nails.

I believed *something different*.

Something clicked. To my knowledge it was not divine intervention. It was not done in a *coming to Jesus meeting*. My pastor did not lay hands on me and pray. My parents did not punish me into changing.

What I believed about my life, mattered.

It was still about me, but what I wanted for me, *changed.*

What's the point? Take a moment and consider what you know about God.

Hold it there.

Because how we see or *how we understand (think about)* God directly influences any explanation of God.

Ready? Let's proceed.

After college, I questioned what I believed about God.

You might ask me, "Wait, you waited until after college to question what you believed about God?"

Not quite. Often, I questioned God and my held beliefs about him.

In a way, I still do. The exception between then and now are the questions which are raised more in hopeful expectation than in hopeless doubt.

However, back when I graduated from college, I was ready to be *done with God*. I knew he existed, but I thought he was *too hard*. I could not reconcile my perception of God's character and his expectations for my life.

I was done.

Thankfully, I did not abandon my pursuit.

It comes down to the angle at which we view something and how we perceive that thing.

Perspective matters as much as perception.

Who is God?

The answer can be simple and that is my aim. Every chapter after this must be understood as something that extends from God.

There are plenty of descriptions we can utilize to answer our question.

The Bible is paramount in describing a *one God system* in a culture that believe there were many gods. The ancient peoples did not have the Internet to help spurn the access of information and consequential perpetuation of doubt of higher beings, because there was so much those people did not know.

The many god system of explanation came about to help people make sense of the world.

At least this is how we can maybe understand their creation. Many Christians believe an all-powerful and intelligent Creator spoke and set our universe in motion. Because science has not adequately offered another more viable solution, the idea of an intelligent designer lives on.

Part of answering *who is God* is to ask and answer *is God real?*

I believe so and here's why: it is a prima facie case. Show me sufficient evidence against God and I will consider your case. C.S. Lewis changed his position from atheist to Christian because when he weighed science and theism, he determined one of the two could fit both in their explanation while the other excludes one. Theism won as science helps reveal God.

For many this may not seem so black and white. It can be difficult explaining shades of gray.

For some people, God is like that. God may exist, but everything after is difficult to reconcile.

For me, the world either started out evil or it started out good.

Call me narrow, but if the God of Christianity is defined as love, then the fact there is love in the world would suggest love has a source and the source is God. I may be disqualifying myself with that position, but bear with me.

Either the world began broken and love rose up to combat it or the world began in love and evil came about to combat it.

The Bible says God is love. If the Bible says it, then there should be an example of it in real life. Let's back up to when I was eight years old.

Around that age I got down on my knees and prayed the magical prayer *inviting Jesus into my heart.*

I grew up in a home that was obligated toward God. However, my family was on the brink of destruction and my innocent little heart was not prepared for what was about to happen.

The relationship between my father and myself, though he was married to my mother, was by all technical terms legally bound.

He partook in the traditional practice of procreation. He and my mother danced the horizontal shuffle and ten months later I entered the world.

Unlike ordering food at the fast-food restaurant, marriage and parenthood bring about many first time experiences of which books upon books are written in an attempt to increase awareness and better prepare folks for these life-long journeys. Ordering fast-food may not be the best example, but generally speaking, you have a hopeful expectation of what you are going to get, regardless of location.

Marriage and parenthood are not like that.

My mother and my father wanted children. They created a child before me. Unfortunately, the child did not come about, as there was a miscarriage.

I did not know the man and woman who went through what I assume to be, a heart-wrenching experience.

That of losing a child.

My wife and I do not like to entertain the thought of *what if we lost our son?* Tricky emotions are those affiliated with losing something that possessed so many dreams and much expectation. The wonder and the impetuous questions beginning with

What if...?

I know others who have experienced this unfortunate valley and have been told it is different for men than it is for women. Men's bodies do not change throughout the nine month process as much as a woman's.

I wonder what my parents were like before then.

They were young.

They were newly married.

They were hopeful.

Their first child was on the way. Then, at some point, it was gone.

How does one move on from that?

I was the second pregnancy.

My father claimed to never be good with kids. Biologically he was my *creator*, but for many years was not my *father*.

Maybe he was scared? They had already lost one child. Maybe he was hesitant to get attached.

My family was not the only family to have been in the situation they were in. My father worked full-time so he was gone most of the time. Even when he was in the house, he was rarely present—interacting and drawing near to me.

On the flip-side, my mother stayed home. We were like two peas in a pod, together all day—everyday.

Why is this important?

Many homes in the 20th and 21st Centuries look like this home.

Ever since the Industrial Revolution, year-by-year more fathers left the home to work in order to provide for their family. The mother was left at home to care for the house and children.

For centuries the family was one cohesive unit. Father and mother present together would form the family. The son watched their father and the daughters learned from their mothers.

However, throughout most of history, fathers ruled in the home. Though both were present, in most cases the father was the king of his domain. Without getting into a long discourse on marital and familial roles, a solid dynamic would look like this:

Man and woman working together, accountable to each other with many of the toughest and final decisions falling to the man unless relegated to the woman.

No dominion.

No hierarchy.

Accountability.

Support.

Things changed.

Starting around the time of the Industrial Revolution, roles started to change. Increasingly, fathers became more absent in the home. Divorce increased at a similar rate. The roles of the father changed from being the main character and model to the co-star. Even more, the role of the father may have fallen to the background as face-to-face interaction with fathers decreased.

Dad leaves the home to work, children spend their days with mom. Dad, seeing his children less, has to catch up with them whenever he can. The scene would progress to reoccurring interactions of:

Dad, can I...?

Just wait until your father gets home, then you will be punished!

My father chalked up his lack of interpersonal skills to his uncertainty around children. He was unable to relate with them. Maybe it had to do with losing a child before me. Mix that experience with a lack of confidence and the reaction is probably going to be negative. Moreover, his role often appeared as a last resort source of discipline.

From my perspective, my father was distant, and whenever he got close, it was to inflict pain.

Poor guy.

There I am, eight years old, the world at my finger-tips. After hearing some message on the depths of hell, I signed my ticket to the pearly gates.

I prayed a simple little prayer and sent it heavenward to the grand-poo-pa of Saviors—a verbal invitation to take up residence in my heart.

Seems a bit odd, but all of this is necessary in answering *who is God?*

As far as I knew, I had a healthy heart. I did not understand it then, but I do now, it was not Jesus who literally came to live in my heart. It was the Holy Spirit by way of delegation. Which made me wonder,

So who is this,

Holy

Spirit?

In a nutshell, many people define the Holy Spirit as the general practitioner of God's heart, ensuring each person is appropriately living a moral lifestyle.

At eight, I locked up the lifetime deal of *salvation*. "I want to go to heaven! I want to be a good person too!" Then for the next fourteen years, I struggled to be the morally upright person the Holy Spirit was supposed to accomplish in me.

The Holy Spirit was supposed to convict me of any wrongdoing and make me see the world differently. Except most of the time God felt distant and difficult to please.

My biggest hurdle in my faith was the one thing I was supposed to have faith in.

The relationship with my father was similar,

distant.

This is not an exact parallel, but close enough for those who lived when Jesus walked the earth. God felt distant. The difference between God of the Old Testament and the God of the New Testament could be boiled down to a God who visited (came and went) and a God who dwells or inhabits.

For those before Jesus, the *law* perpetuated this visitational interaction with God.

If God created me, then he gave me his spirit to guide and take care of me, and so I tried my best to always do right by God and make him happy.

My relationship was legally bound.

Sure, I have salvation locked up because of Jesus and all, but I did my best to avoid the metaphysical thrashing awaiting me if I decide to indulge in physical temptation or defy various church traditions.

My mindset was simple. If I can make God happy by my actions then conversely, I can make him angry.

Does this resonate?

Dave Kinnaman noted in his book *unChristian*, "Our research consistently underscores this reality: efforts to connect people to God are frequently undermined by the lasting negative influences of absent, abusive, or negligent parents."

Who is God?

God

is

Father.

O.M.F.?

Can I stop there?

How would you describe God?

What are some words you would use to describe the *perfect* father?

Good.

Kind.

Trustworthy.

Understanding.

Empathetic.

Nurturing.

Comforting.

Righteous.

Teacher.

Coach.

Faithful.

Gracious.

Partial toward me.

Just.

Protecting.

Powerful.

Unstoppable.

Fierce.

Violent.

Loving.

A father helps create the child and displays love for the child through the context of his marriage what the he thinks of the world. He is the embodiment of love.

He disciplines his children. He does not punish or condemn them. He is fierce and violent toward evil. The father and mother in tandem seek to protect the child. However, they know they cannot protect the child against all instances of hurt or pain.

We are all children.

I am not the illegitimate love-child of a cosmic accident.

Think about the ideal mother. How many words would cross over from the short list we made for *father*?

God is the embodiment of all things *good*.

This is what so many people struggle with, is God real or merely a created philosophical idea?

Who is God?

The Bible is extremely helpful in learning about God and his acts, but one must *experience* his *ways*. One must encounter God's *presence*. I can understand why it is hard to really give any more time or thought to him.

How we see God, matters.

Unfortunately, there are many people who think they need to defend God or simply,

be right.

If it is true we are children of God, then there are a lot of people misrepresenting him. I want to be transparent and say,

I apologize.

That's the kicker though, isn't it?

Rarely can I find someone who has a negative thing to say about Jesus. Maybe I am talking to the wrong people. There are plenty of people who have negative things to say about God or Christians.

There are plenty of Christians who will speak for God and claim God is out to destroy all evil…people.

God is out for blood. Either jump on the Jesus train or get left at the station.

I believe God is out *looking for us.*

He has always been that way.

God is either for us or against us.

How we see it directly impacts our experience.

Brennan Manning said, "Whenever faith is accepted merely as a closed system of well-defined doctrines, we lost contact with the living God."

God is experience.

Unless we experience his nature, hope for a joyful or transformed life is lost.

What we believe about his nature will impact our experience.

And sometimes, in our narrow-mindedness, we catch a glimpse of God's kindness and it changes our perspective. Our mindset undergoes a transformation.

Chapter 3:
Transparency &
A Weak Literary Transition

Have you ever watched the movie *Forrest Gump?*

The following story was my Lieutenant Dan type of moment.

I was not on a boat, but I was in what felt like a sea of emotions. The perfect storm was not upon me, but I was in a yelling match with God. It was a full moon and I was on a walk with God in a cornfield behind my dormitory. I cannot remember what year of college it was, but something was so pressing on my mind I had to get out and take a walk.

The walk took me east from my dorm toward a recently harvested cornfield.

I was angry.

Part of me thinks I was heartbroken over some female. In melodramatic fashion I must have envisioned the performance of a lifetime. I needed answers and my emotional interaction in front of God was going to warrant those answers.

I attended Lincoln Christian College. Since then its name has been changed to Lincoln Christian University. It is in small town U.S.A. Central Illinois. However, I am from Chicagoland. For those of us who live in northern Illinois, anything south of Interstate 80 is considered *Southern Illinois.* Upon arriving to Lincoln I spoke with the locals and they explained the difference between my understanding and their understanding. It probably would have helped if I had actually looked at a map of Illinois because Lincoln is not far from the geographical center of Illinois, maybe fifteen miles.

In Lincoln, the only thing open *after hours* would have been the 24-hour Steak-n-Shake restaurant. I must have been broke because I could have used a burger and a shake, but on that night the fries would have to wait.

Imagine the scene.

The camera would start with a first person perspective of the floor and follow me as I move through the hall toward the door. It would cut to a distance shot of me exiting the northeast wing in the direction where we would occasionally hit golf balls. The cornfield was an easy quarter mile from where my trip started.

Hans Zimmer would probably pass on the opportunity to compose the score for this scene. Let's assume he entertained the idea as he opens with some harsh riffs on some stringed instruments with some bellowing drums. The camera pans around to track my seemingly solo march toward existential enlightenment. The music puts you, the viewer, in a place where you cannot even track your own emotions.

Intense.

My thoughts like a tidal wave quickly escalate to tsunami status. There were no buoys to predict this kind of mental, emotional, or spiritual movement. Drama.

It was a full moon.

If I remember right, I felt a strange itch behind my ears and an increased sensitivity to scents. My hair started to grow at a rapid rate—

just kidding.

As I reach the cornfield stumbling to and fro from the uneven terrain, my breakdown begins. A middle class white kid attending a small Christian liberal arts college in one of the richest countries in the world, blessed with an above average athletic ability accompanied by an above average intelligence with a side order of A.D.H.D began to berate the Creator of the universe.

About something I now can only guess what was the topic.

Ridiculous.

What in the world do I need to be yelling at God about?

Both of my parents were alive. I never suffered from a life-threatening illness. Materialistically speaking, I was alright. I had a solid group of friends. From the outside, I was normal.

From the inside?

I was a mess.

I spent an hour or so yelling at God about whatever. I truly cannot remember what it was. It must not have been important because the content of the monologue is not stored within reach of my immediate recall. It was after this recurring tantrum of theological ignorance I called it a night and began the walk back to the dorm. I needed to stop thinking.

As I attempted to stop thinking and give my mind a break, something incredible happened. It was within fifty feet of the building, the same door through which I began this journey some uninitiated words spilled from my mouth.

I know it wasn't me. It kind of freaked me out. I do not believe it was some Freudian subconscious consolation for the desperation I felt in the cold of night.

There I was walking and the moment I stopped thinking my mouth said,

"It will be O.K."

I won't pretend to say what you're thinking. Take it for what you think it is worth, but this was the first time I can confirm I heard the audible voice of God. The first time I really *felt his presence.*

I had no other explanation. I did not feel in control of my body.

Call me, *crazy.*

I guess I *felt* as much as a human could feel a theoretically made up being.

But, God is *intentional.*

This all-powerful, all-knowing, ever-present being requires what on the surface appears to be an incredible amount of faith.

Answering the question of *who is God* involves asking a follow-up question, *if God is _____, then what does that mean for me?*

I never read it, but books like Rick Warren's *Purpose Driven Life* had sold over an estimated 25 million copies. That does not include the amount of times a donated copy is sold at a thrift store. I heard somewhere that some 80% of Americans identify with some form of Christianity, the whole belief in God, stuff.

The cynic that used to live in me asks, really?

Over 240 million Americans believe in an all-powerful, all-knowing, ever-present being who may or may not rely on faith for its power, and the United States appears to be laden with chaos?

No way.

The child of God in me asks, *do all of those people believe God believes in them?*

Does God purpose life in people?

I think he does.

I think he purposes life in every person.

Let's back up to the story of creation and work from there.

Chapter 4:
Starting Points

The first book of the Bible begins with "In the beginning…"

I imagine God, in the void and the darkness thinking, "I could really turn this into something."

The way the story goes, when there was *nothing* there was God and angels.

Angels were everywhere. God is also everywhere.

Sounds crowded.

Picture God sitting on his throne, one by one placing angels on the head of a pin. Behind him there is what would appear to be an insurmountable pile of really big rocks.

I believe God has a sense humor. Archangel Michael? Doubtful.

Why did God start creating things?

God is perfect.

Assuming God is perfect would imply that God does not lack anything. That means when God got to creating, he was not creating to fill a void or right an imbalance.

Or was he?

Depends on what you have heard about the fall of Lucifer.

Genesis 1:1-2 says "In the beginning, God created the heavens and the earth. The earth was without form and void, and darkness was over the face of the deep."

My fault, there was both void and darkness.

What about Lucifer? Did he become *Satan* before or after creation?

Lucifer was really close to God. Along the way, I think Lucifer became jealous of God. Lucifer wanted a lot of things, but one of those things is something that is only reserved for God, and that thing is worship. I don't talk much about worship in this book. However, there was a severe disagreement between God and Lucifer. A battle ensued resulting in Lucifer's damnation. There were some other angels who went with him.

Let's pretend the disagreement was over God's plan for creation. Lucifer took issue with it. God saw void and wanted to fill it with something new. Where he saw darkness he wanted to fill it with light.

God got to creating for the sake of creation. To create is to make life.

In a way, by creating the world and creating humankind, God put himself out there. God made himself vulnerable.

The universe is old. Super old. The earth is old too. How old? Does it matter? I think there is enough evidence to suggest the earth has been around many years before life inhabited it.

What was part of God's creative process? What things did he almost include, but then decide to leave out? Anyone else wonder this same thought?

When I was a kid, I spent hours playing with legos. This was in the 90's. Legos were growing in popularity. In the 21st century, legos became larger than life. They have their own stores and even *lego art* in museums. There are even lego movies. This would have made the child version of myself go nuts.

There have been other building sets like lincoln logs and tinker toys. I know erector sets were popular too. Among creative toys nothing has had the same prominence as legos. Some bright individual even created a digital version of legos. They may be offended by that statement, but Minecraft allows similar creating in a digital space with users collectively logging over 2 billion hours of playtime on Xbox Live in two years!

Incredible.

I had dreams to be awesome with legos. I wanted to do things like the students who built a full-functioning car out of legos. However, I lacked the engineering savvy.

Creating is built into our DNA.

I love creating. I still do. It seemed easier to create with reckless abandon when in elementary school. I am blessed with a photographic-like memory. It got me through school with a relative amount of ease. My relationship with creating directly impacts my perspective of God.

In second grade, my teacher called my mother to discuss my behavior at school. Like any involved mother, she asked the teacher about my grades. This conversation happened, but the following dialogue is somewhat conjecture:

    My teacher said, "Oh Nolan's grades are fine," assuring my mother, "but it is the children who sit around Nolan that worries me."

    Confused, my mother asked "Why then are you calling?"

    "Well, the thing is I cannot explain why Nolan's marks are so good. While I teach, I catch him drawing, cutting paper, often he will glue things, kind of like he is doing some sort of craft. All of this happens in the small opening of his desk where he does not think I can see him. Then I watch the children that also see what he is doing and those are the ones that are struggling. See, although Nolan is doing well, he is distracting the other children."

    "Is he being disruptive?" My mother said, trying not to be offended.

    "Not in the way a child normally disrupts class. I wanted to let you know that I took those things away during times when I am teaching, so that way he cannot distract the others."

My mother understood. I say all this because I am not a famous architect, which is probably due to my second grade teacher. That is logical, right?

My mind is always moving like that. It never quits, always watching, absorbing, deciphering and manifesting the things I picture. Legos played a large role in channeling those creative juices.

I think I learned it from God. His infinite ideas on creation is difficult to harness from a finite perspective. There is no comparison between re-creation and creation.

Reenacting history or forming it.

I wonder if, on some level God felt that way.

At some point, he just started creating things. Little by little, no rush or deadline, God began to piece together universes with building blocks way more complicated than legos. Maybe those building blocks are like legos to God. In what limited knowledge we have garnered from studying the earth, NASA has determined the earth has an atmosphere, lithosphere, hydrosphere, cryosphere, and biosphere.

I have not the faintest idea what each *sphere* means, but NASA compares these interacting systems with those of the human body. Each contains independent and interacting systems that rely on each other. Let's call it an interdependent system.

The earth's atmosphere is comprised mostly of nitrogen, about 78 percent, and 21 percent is oxygen. The other one percent is a mixture of various gases. Theoretically, if the mixture were any different, human life would not exist on the earth.

The earth is tilted at 23.45 degrees, with the same idea in place, tilt it backward or forward another degree and life would not exist. Do any internet search on earth composition and let the facts bore or overwhelm you.

After the universes were formed it got to the point God wanted to create something or someone like himself. The Bible says God created humans *in his image*. I never used legos to build a lego-based likeness of me. It would look too rigid and not compliment my boyish looks and soft edges.

I think there is something within the heart of God that was not satisfied. It was not until after he created every other living creature humans came around. And I wonder, the other biological beings were created from the dust of the earth, but God did not breath life into them. I mean, the creation narrative is definitely poetic, but is it metaphorical, literal, or both?

Is mankind *of* the earth,

or is mankind *from* the earth.

Again, is it both?

I find it hard to believe God created man to worship His grand mastery status as the Creator of all things. If there are such things as angels, then what is said about them in the Bible describes the roles of angels as servants. These beings live to glorify and serve God. Even then, it could be misconstrued God is insecure and needs to be constantly reaffirmed as if he is some kind of fairy. If enough people did not believe him, then God will die and Nietzsche may finally get quoted within an appropriate context!

I doubt God has a meter gauging humanity's active belief in God. Furthermore, angels do not appear to be mindless drones. The goodness of God must be so great, the angels cannot help but worship.

For God, humans served a different purpose.

We are the perfect synthesis of free-will and interdependence.

God can do anything within himself. Humanity by design is able to do incredible things too. God knew what it means to be like him. He made it so life must extend from him.

As much as Cathy Lee may not need Regis, so too man does not need God and God does not need humans, but when they collaborate, the possibilities would blow us away.

The Bible said God charged man, not with a crime, but with a calling to take this wonderful gift we know as the earth and to cultivate life on it. God started small with Adam—his name in Hebrew means *beginning* or simply *mankind*. He was given a small plot of land on the upper east side with a deluxe apartment in the sky—Eden. Adam's 9 to 5 grind was a simple one: walk with God and learn his ways. Other activities included naming some animals and to strategically expand the garden's perimeter.

God's love for food was also introduced at this time when he filled the garden with many fruit-bearing trees.

And in the name of free-will, God provided at least one alternative to everything God gave Adam. We identify this tree as the *Tree of Knowledge* or a longer name, *Tree of the Knowledge of Good and Evil*.

I do not know the duration of each day in the creation narrative as there is much speculation on the subject. Frankly, I don't think it matters.

Adam lived alone in the garden for a time. How long? I do not know. Adam interacted with the animals, but that was only entertaining for a time.

However, God foresaw and experienced it would be good for Adam to also have a counterpart, much like mankind is to God and vice versa.

Enter, Eve.

Adam is to mankind what Eve is to *beginning* or *mother of all*.

It is as if man is the curator and protector and woman is the gateway to life or shoe shopping, but we will go with life, because it sounds better.

God created the world for Adam and Adam for the world. The world was not enough so God created Eve.

Eve was the gateway to life. Life could be cultivated through the relationship between Adam and Eve. Adam could have ignored Eve, but instead he woke up and said "Finally, someone like me."

Eve can be seen as a metaphor for our standing as mankind in the eyes of God.

If Adam is a representation of God and Eve is a representation of people, God looks on us with similar understanding, "Finally, someone like me."

Unfortunately, the glory of it all was interrupted by *sin*. We will discuss sin in the next chapter, but here let me describe what God intended and what sin interrupted in the relationship between man and woman.

For far too long woman have suffered at the hands of men.

Here's why: men *feared* women.

An ancient understanding of fear is to *have a divided mind about something.* If there is any doubt in our minds about the definition or purpose of something, then a feeling wells up inside of us, unsure of how to see and understand the object—that's *fear.*

Is it common for us to control what we don't understand?

Call it what you like, but I am talking about perspective. The position from which we view something.

I think men *feared* women. Some think it should be present tense, but things are changing.

Backing up for a moment.

At what point did women become *lower* than men? In many cultures men still look down on women.

Is it their generally smaller physical frame or muscle volume?

Is it their predisposition to be kind and compassionate?

What makes men so *mighty?*

Is it because men are generally larger?

Is it their predisposition to be feel strong and desire respect?

Sometimes, we cannot find the right answer simply because we are asking the wrong questions.

The Biblical description of *woman* in the book of Genesis gives us a more detailed picture.

I grew up in a home where my main caretaker was my mother. My mother was the representation of strength and kindness. She was also the provider and disciplinarian. I was the only man in a house full of females. You could say I struggled to stay afloat in an ocean of estrogen.

My family life was common, more common than a home led by a mother and a father. Today, my wife and I throw around the word *partner* when talking about our corresponding relationship.

Partner implies a certain level of interdependence.

The writer of Genesis describes how God saw it was not good for Adam to be alone. When the animals did not fill the role, God created Eve. Assuming the account in Genesis is somewhat literal, the text says Adam fell into a "deep sleep." The picture is different than popping an Ambien and taking a long awaited snooze.

Deep sleep is a possible mixture of a coma, trance, or a deathlike lethargy—an inability to move.

Ancient languages have a complex system of words that built off of or combined words to better communicate something. At least this is how it tends to look from our position looking backwards into history. There are layers of meaning in words demanding us to pay close attention. These layers present an interesting task, for our modern understanding may need to change from time to time because of ongoing investigation and discovery of new information.

Furthermore, it can be argued each person sees the world in direct comparison to their own life circumstances and experience. Smart people call this *associative learning*.

Our brain does its best to give meaning and understanding to new information and experiences. Often times, our previous experiences and knowledge impede the acquisition of new information by associating the information with something close to, but not at all identical to the thing we are receiving.

For example, my nephew learned the word "dog." It sounds more like "gog," but he uses that word whenever he is referring to any animal with four legs.

So *deep sleep* in Genesis 2 isn't exactly what you may consider to be *deep sleep* in the 21st century. And *woman* in the 21st century may not be the same *woman* from Genesis 2.

God saw something in the creation of women that was intended to be something incredible, amazing, and awesome. The relationship between God and Adam was a dynamic unique to itself, but in creating *woman*, God took it to another level.

The relationship between man and woman was not supposed to be the work many claim it is today. An intimate relationship with someone else requires work.

God call Eve a *help-mate*.

What is a help-mate?

Help-mate comes from two Hebrew words with roots and cultural contexts that help us with a different definition.

Eve was to be an equal partner with a significant amount of power.

I found a literal translation that reads, God created *a power to face* Adam.

In other places of the Old Testament the same word used for *help* is used to classify the strength or aid God lends in a time of need.

The historical context of *mate* is the literal understanding of someone able to look another person in the eye. Neither person has to look down or up to make eye contact. They stand at equal height and can without adjustment see each other.

In the name of combining words we get *help-mate.*

In the name of understanding we should use the phrase *a power to face Adam.*

Man and woman created as equals but with similar and corresponding abilities.

I guess it is a matter of what one believes.

Perspective matters.

God purposed something in how he created man and woman. The purposes of creation and humankind were interrupted by the choices of Adam and Eve. But he saw something beautiful in the inevitable mess that would become humankind so he made them anyways.

So lets talk more about the mess.

CHAPTER 5:
Well This is Awkward

What about sin?

In my mind, I always sought to be the good kid.

I do not remember how that got instilled in me, maybe a psychologist would have a solid explanation since I am the oldest child, but I do remember having an incredible fear of making God angry.

There was a period of my life where I believed if I forgot to ask God for forgiveness for all of the sins known and unknown of that day then hell would await me upon my untimely nocturnal death. I would hope God would have mercy on me so I could live to see another day and further hope to make him happy and bring him honor.

Whenever I would mess up, on purpose, I would wonder, *just how bad is this? Will God forgive this action?*

I felt God's grace was given out of obligation. That God and Jesus discussed saving humanity, but God did not want to sacrifice his only son, so he told Jesus he could not come to earth. Then in an act of bravery, Jesus came to earth and died on the cross anyway. Then maybe God told the Apostle John to write at least three chapters and sixteen verses of what people would call a gospel.

Could God really say he loved someone and then send them to hell for not asking for forgiveness each day?

The Bible says God loved us because he sent Jesus. My understanding of this love was a little off.

He created us, right?

So he had to put up with us and the only way to justifiably put up with our shenanigans and maintain order was for Jesus to die and satisfy the rules.

It was nailed into my being to self-identify with the phrase, *I am a sinner.*

Some people who think they understand grace on a deeper level say, I *am a sinner…saved by grace.*

I am unsure exactly what happened the day Eve ate the forbidden fruit. What in the garden was Adam thinking as he idly stood by and gawked while this magnificent creature succulently pierced the side of that fruit with her seemingly gorgeous teeth and luscious lips?

Sorry if this got awkward. Just trying to understand how Adam dropped the ball and let sin into the world.

God is not big on *rules.*

That is how things started out. He is more about relationships and healthy lifestyle choices. He told Adam and Even they could eat of every tree in the garden which included the Tree of Life; but they could not eat of the Tree of the Knowledge of Good and Evil.

Sin, if it is an actual thing, has always existed.

The Bible said sin entered the cosmos through Adam. This cosmos would have been the known world—all of existence. Like discovering a new use for an everyday thing, sin was there all along, but in regards to us, it did not yet exist.

Sin.

The kind of word that creates awkward silence or ceaseless chatter. There seems to be no in-between when it comes to the topic of sin.

It kind of annoys me like a fly stuck between the blinds and a closed window. The buzzing and the thunk-thunk-thunk against the window can make a person go crazy.

A lot of Christians talk about sin. Like all the time, like a teenager, like with a limited vocabulary will like, talk like, about sin like.

Look at a Google Ngram concerning the frequency of the word sin and you will see a steady decline from the 1800's until the 21st century only to see it is back on the upswing.

The modern understanding of the word *sin* came from the mix of an Old English word and a Latin word.

Growing up I struggled to differentiate between the pronunciation of shoulder and soldier. In those days, I was more easily embarrassed. It makes my shoulders shudder to think of my mispronunciation of a girl giving me the cold soldier.

Maybe that is what happened with the word *sin*. Or maybe not, but to me the general English understanding of the word *sin* is a far cry from words used in the Hebrew and Greek.
Chatah is pronounced ka-tah with the *k* having a bit of saliva in the back of your throat sound. Chatah is the transliterated version of the Hebrew word.

Simply, chatah can mean to forget ones standing or position, miss the mark. We have to be careful in translating ancient language, but chatah has multiple interpretations. There are areas where it describes immense guilt. The challenge is to avoid settling on an extreme in an effort to have a solidified definition. Generations of pastors have hung their hat on the definition of immense guilt.

To be fair, sin is what many pastors explained to me as a moral wrongdoing against God. People taught me all humans are sinful and need to repent of their sins and turn to Jesus. I heard the story about Adam and Eve. I learned about Lucifer, Satan, and Voldemort.

These same people inflated the eating of the forbidden fruit like it was pedophilia or murder.

Because of how people taught me to look at and understand sin, I grew up a Christian living in fear for my soul. It took years before I learned something did not match up.

I asked questions:

Why did God create mankind?

Why did God create a tree no one was supposed to touch?

Why did God allow Lucifer to live and not obliterate him?

Why did sin matter so much?

The Bible says one day Lucifer will be entirely destroyed. I think God wanted to show him how bad Lucifer missed it. God would not be crossed by an angel.

God has a whole system set up. We may not see it in its entirety, but we catch glimpses of it here on earth. Because of this, we need to leave the inflated understanding of sin behind and seek a new perspective.

If God created man for the sake of life so man could enjoy it and God; then God would not have to set up a double standard requiring mankind's allegiance.

There are plenty of people who do not enjoy either the world or God.

There are some who are too afraid to really live and some who are too afraid to die.

Then there are those who enjoy the fruit of their labor; rind, pulp and all.

A full relationship requires choice.

Sin is the missing of the target in the relationship.

If my wife felt forced to love me and held this perception her entire life, then she could grow bitter. There is a reason arranged marriages get a different rap than modern marriage. Many people in arranged marriages must choose how they will interact with their spouse. They can aim at love or bitterness.

God could have arranged mankind's requirement to worship a deity. The angels are responsible for strict service and worship. The God of Judaism and consequently Christianity is supposed to be different than any other God...*ever*.

Pagan gods required worship. God has a slightly different standard.

God is about fullness of life.

We are not required to worship, but it is highly recommended and strongly encouraged.

Worship benefits the worshipper. God does not need it, but we do.

He created mankind with a choice to enjoy God in everything good. This meant having something to not choose.

Our understanding of chatah is backed up in the narrative of Genesis. The serpent questioned Adam and Eve about God's instructions, "Did God really say, 'You can't eat from any tree in the garden'?"

They remembered what God said and responded accordingly, "The woman said to the serpent, "We may eat the fruit from the trees in the garden. But about the fruit of the tree in the middle of the garden, God said, 'You must not eat it or touch it, or you will die.'"

The serpent twisted God's words and targeted their perspective, "No! You will not die," the serpent said to the woman. "In fact, God knows that when you eat it your eyes will be opened and you will be like God, knowing good and evil."

Adam and Eve were quick to remember God's word and then they were quick to forget,

> "Then the woman saw that the tree was good for food and delightful to look at, and that it was desirable for obtaining wisdom. So she took some of its fruit and ate it; she also gave some to her husband, who was with her, and he ate it. Then the eyes of both of them were opened, and they knew they were naked; so they sewed fig leaves together and made loincloths for themselves."

They had a special standing with God. Upon eating the fruit, they saw there were other positions. In one action Adam and Eve forgot God and directly defied his instruction.

To directly defy someone would be considered a *transgression*. The Old Testament Word is *pesha*. The New Testament uses the word *paraptoma*. The Bible uses the word *chatah* to describe Adam and Eve's action and not *pesha*.

What's the point?

People taught me all sin is a direct defiance of God. To them, sin is a black and white issue. In a way, it is.

In another way, not so much. It is black and white, I either remember God or I don't remember him. However, when do I know if I am forgetting God?

The Apostle Paul wrote, "All unrighteousness is sin." This is also the same person who said, "Righteousness comes by faith alone." I talk more about *faith* in chapter nine, but here it discusses *believing the validity of something.*

So, if I don't believe God then I am committing sin.

If I fully comprehended the goodness of God and his intentions for me, would I ever forget him?

Would I sin?

Sin is different than *just* wronging someone. If I pull into a parking spot and neglect to stop in time and hit the car in the next spot, I have wronged the owner. It is not that I forgot about the person or neglected to consider their feelings, but I did *forget* to press the brake pedal.

In a way then, because I forgot to press the pedal I wronged the person by colliding with their vehicle.

The problem is the focus on the word *sin* instead of what is behind it.

All sin is evil even if it is does not appear to come from a root of evil. This is the unfortunate, but brighter side to sin.

It sucks to consider murdering someone is just as evil as unintentionally hitting someone's car. It is what it is.

The bright side is the redemption available to anyone who sins. Our purpose here is to redirect our held perspective of sin and change our focus. Talking about which sin is worse than another in the scheme of the cosmos is a lose-lose conversation.

It is exactly what the serpent would want, "Did God really say…"

I grew up in the Lutheran church. From what I learned, sin was something to avoid, but the only direction I was pointed in was to worship God and make him happy. The catch is God will get angry with every sin I do not confess. I was not taught how the role of sin changed after Jesus died and rose from the dead.

Jesus should have become the main character and focus of the conversation. This happened in the first church too as recorded in the book of Acts, but many Jewish Christians would say, "Yeah! Jesus!" then default back to "Now because of Jesus, stop sinning and follow the law."

The conversation we have today is very similar to what was discussed in the first century. Many people ended up saying "Forget it!" This was me. Maybe you said some of these things,

"What does it matter? I cannot change."

"This is just who I am…"

"Maybe I was born this way…"

"No one is righteous"

It's exhausting.

Have you ever lugged around a dead body? Sounds like a lot of work.

This is sin. The serpent wants us to lug the conversation of sin around like a dead body.

The more one talks about sin the less they talk about Jesus.

So sin becomes inflated. The serpent twists the conversation. He wants to usurp our position and purpose.

Instead of being people created to enjoy life, our identity gets questioned. One pastor described it this way, "Satan does not whisper in your ear, 'you are this…' or 'you are that…' instead his whispers are disguised as my thoughts:

I am a pervert.

I am a whore.

I am no good.

I am unlovable.

I am not that bad.

I am a sinner.

I am alone.

We allowed the conversation of *Jesus* to get hijacked by *sin*.

I can ignore the whispers until I acknowledge them as true. Once I make them my own, I become whatever it is I repeat.

The Bible says to "be wise of what is good, yet innocent about what is evil."

I wish I did not know the slightest thing about evil. I wish I did not understand it. Before understanding more about Jesus and all of that, I wish I did not feel like dirt whenever I experienced a perverted or malicious thought.

Forgetting God allowed the relationship to be interrupted. It created confusion.

Adam and Eve forgot God's love and their eyes were opened to fear. Their prefrontal cortexes were flooded with all of these seemingly contradictory ideas demanding rationality. Their brains were incapable of the task.

Was God good or was he evil?

Was the serpent evil?

"Wow, Eve, when did you get that mole?"

"Adam, for the last time will you floss! There's corn in your teeth!"

Immediately there was separation between humankind and God;

they thought, *am I naked?*

Adam in the first of a total dude moment blames God and Eve;

"The woman *YOU* gave to be with me—*SHE* gave me some fruit from the tree, and I ate."

Sin entered the earth through this situation many Christians call *The Fall.*

Adam and Eve chose something other than God and in so doing acquired a new self-awareness God did not desire for Adam and Eve to possess.

God instructed them not to eat of one tree for consequences he foresaw because of the system set in place in the cosmos. The instruction was not because *God said so.*

God created Adam and Eve for relationship.

God related with Adam and Adam with God.

Adam related with nature and nature with Adam.

Adam related himself.

Adam related with Eve and Eve with Adam.

The struggle is real when sin dominates our focus.

I used to consistently see myself as a disappointment to God.

I understood little about my inner battles.

Forgetting God and aiming for something else brought about confusion on a global scale. It does not help when sin hijacks the conversation and is disguised, misinterpreted and inflated in the Western Church.

Sin was a problem, but Jesus is the solution.

This solution came through *covenant*, God's blood connection to us.

CHAPTER 6:
Tom Sawyer & Huck Finn Theology

I have heard this line various places,

"With every ending comes a new beginning."

The book of Genesis has both beginnings and endings.

There are some things we learn about beginnings and endings in the first three chapters and into the seventh chapter.

Earlier, I mentioned the Bible opens with the words, "In the beginning…"

Our world had a beginning. And until Adam and Eve decided to get curious and gain *the knowledge of good and evil*, there was no intention of Adam and Eve ever dying or this world ever coming to an end.

Genesis 3 describes this fall of man. God said what was intended to be, and by "to be" I mean to always be, never-ending, would eventually have an end.

Death entered the world.

Yet, humankind continued to multiply. The Bible describes humankind's actions as increasing in opposition to God. There are even descriptions of women mixing with fallen angels and creating giants and other larger than life humans.

Interestingly, the Bible is not the only book to describe these super humans. When was the last time you discussed this in Sunday School?

God saw humankind did not desire God. What did not help was the life God breathed into Adam was a life force.

Humans lives for hundreds of years! Or so the Bible says.

Eventually, God grew depressed with the sad state of affairs that became of his wonderful creation. God has standards, any reasonable being would. God decided to start over. The greater part of the population ended up getting annihilated by an insurmountable amount of water described to us in the seventh chapter.

The world was given a new beginning. This guy, Noah, and his family were chosen to lead this new world and start over.

Some thoughts spring to mind. In the first chapter, we read God created the heavens and the earth.

I can assume there was nothing before he created things.

For some reason, and for one of many reasons I cannot understand, God decided to create things and he did it without my trusted legos or any proverbial building blocks. He created the building blocks of life out of nothing.

After God wiped out all but a couple handfuls of people with the flood, He used the same world of which to let things start again. He is God, he does what he pleases. He could have easily started over and no one would have been wiser. But, He is God. So, there's that.

Here is what I know; there is something in this story we can learn about the heart of God and how covenant and grace works.

Grace is not about elimination of what was and creating something new.

Grace is not about wiping the slate clean. It is not about grabbing a new canvas.

God started the world over by using people who were present before the great flood. He did not create a new foundation of the world, he kept it and changed the guard.

That's it.

God did not re-create anything. He moved some pieces around the board and let mankind have a go at it again.

What about covenant?

God is all about this thing, *covenant*.

There is a difference between a covenant and a contract. Maybe an example from my days in the fourth grade will help our cause.

In the fourth grade me and two friends decided to ask out three girls. Shake your head with me as I type this. How do fourth graders date each other?

One of the girls was the principal's daughter, a girl I was in love with. Previously, in first grade I got down on one knee and had proclaimed my love to her. Hilarious.

The three of us were the Three Amigos or the Three Stooges and they were Monica, Rachel, and Phoebe or the Golden Girls.

O.K. maybe not the Golden Girls.

Every so often the school would put on these roller skating parties at the roller rink in a neighboring town. I could not roller skate to save my life. My family was slow to the popularization of the inline skate, so suffice it to say my first few parties were mostly spent walking slowly on the traditional roller skates between the concession stand and the arcade area. I can hear Céline Dion playing, what sweet memories.

The night I am referring to involved inline skates. I was rocking the inline skates and I had become quite talented. I could jump and skate across the circular shaped benches that lined the outside of the rink. Somehow, and my memory does not serve me the pleasure of all the details, but the news got out the three of us wanted to discuss with the three of them how wanted to talk about dating each other. Nothing say romance like, "Hey you want to date? I won't have my driver's license for another six years. Let's do this!"

The conversation did not go exactly like that, but it was eerily similar when we met in the corner of the rink in the exact spot I would, three months down the line yell to my future *ex-girlfriend,* "Hey! I think we should break-up!"

The three of us formed a *contract* with the other three girls. We all decided who liked who and we went on our merry way. What do fourth graders do when they date? I think I got to hold her hand during couple's skate. Or maybe, I was allowed to think about holding her hand during couple's skate? It's whatever.

The contract was pretty weak, but we were ten years old.

Now if we were to have formed a *covenant*, then the relationship may have looked different.

The covenant thing is important to Christianity. It teaches us a lot about God and what we are to believe about God. Covenants and contracts are similar, but different. Covenants are to never to be broken.

Contracts are negotiable.

Contracts break.

Contracts expire.

God created Adam and made a *covenant* with him.

A covenant is something not sealed with a pen, but a life-force held together by blood.

There was no distinction, no seam; it is a life for a life type of bond. God and Adam became blood brothers, so to speak.

In a way, God was Tom and Adam was Huckleberry.

Covenant and contract are similar because the parties have to agree on something.

God chose to enter into covenant with Adam. However, Adam and Eve may not have fully understood covenant. Those two naked people broke their end of the covenant. Never mind they were connected, life for a life, but Adam and Eve chose something else. When this happened, God treated Adam and Eve like you would a child whom unintentionally hurt themselves because they did not trust when you said not to touch the hot pan on the stove.

His response was caring. His response toward the serpent was wrath. God remained committed to them. Sadly, things were set in motion that would have to play out for a time.

Not entirely sure how many years passed before Noah, but by the time God was exhausted with the state of affairs, he bolstered his covenant with man through Noah. God did not destroy the entire world and start from nothing again because he is faithful to his creation.

Destroying everything would have meant breaking the bond.

In the cosmic order of things, it is the way it is.

How do we reconcile God destroying most of the known world and saving a select few? What little I do know from the accounts I have read is Noah and his family were the last real people left on earth who remained faithful to the covenant.

For a long time I was concerned with upsetting God, pushing him to the point of def-con five and my imminent destruction.

As if I have that much influence.

God is so patient and long-suffering he bolstered and reinforced the covenant with multiple people.

Eventually, it fell to Jesus to fulfill the other end of the covenant.

I am getting ahead of myself, but I have learned that because of Jesus and what he accomplished,

I have immense influence on the cosmic order.

I have influence because of the covenant confirmed by the work of Jesus, so in discussing covenant we need to look at Jesus.

But before moving on to Jesus, we will look at the Ten Commandments—the original list on *How To Live The Good Life.*

CHAPTER 7:
The Good, The Bad, & Charlton Heston, again?

Let's discuss the Ten Commandments.

The first instance of the stone tablets can be found in Exodus chapter 20.

God spoke,

I am the Lord your God, who brought you out of the land of Egypt, out of the place of slavery.
1) *Do not have other gods besides Me.*
2) *Do not make an idol for yourself, whether in the shape of anything in the heavens above or on the earth below or in the waters under the earth. You must not bow down to them or worship them; for I, the Lord your God, am a jealous God, punishing the children for the father's sin, to the third and fourth generations of those who hate Me, but showing faithful love to a thousand generations of those who love Me and keep My commands.*
3) *Do not misuse the name of the Lord your God, because the Lord will not leave anyone unpunished who misuses His name.*
4) *Remember the Sabbath day, to keep it holy: You are to labor six days and do all your work, but the seventh day is a Sabbath to the Lord your God. You must not do any work—you, your son or daughter, your male or female slave, your livestock, or the foreigner who is within your gates. For the Lord made the heavens and the earth, the sea, and everything in them in six days; then He rested on the seventh day. There the Lord blessed the Sabbath day and declared it holy.*
5) *Honor your father and your mother so that you may have a long life in the land the Lord your God is giving you.*
6) *Do not murder.*
7) *Do not commit adultery.*
8) *Do not steal.*
9) *Do not give false testimony against your neighbor.*
10) *Do not covet your neighbor's house. Do not covet your neighbor's wife, his male or female slave, his ox or donkey, or anything that belongs to your neighbor.*

I am not much of a list person, but my wife is a list person. I prefer the whole, *I can remember it and if I do not remember it when I need to recall it, then it is not meant to be.*

I think my success rate in that process is low. I have to write lists and set reminders or I forget.

How did we get the Ten Commandments?

Why the *Ten Commandments?*

God created that covenant with Adam. Adam did not do so well with it, but God remained faithful.

Eventually, humankind multiplied and distanced themselves from God. The world became an *evil* place. A far cry from the intentions of Eden. God was going to start over, but instead adhered to whatever cosmic order was in place and kept the covenant with humankind through a man named Noah, who was also a descendent of Adam. So, ipso-facto; the covenant was still with Adam.

Sneaky God.

Or honorable God, sticking with a previously failed people.

After Noah, time carried on.

The earth refilled with people and another man came along in the same familial line whose name was Abram. Abram's story—when seen from a healthy perspective, packs a lot of encouragement and life lessons, but in short: Abram had a wife, they couldn't have a baby, an angel told him his descendants would rival that of the stars, they had a baby, God wanted Abram to kill that baby, then before Abram killed the baby, God stopped Abram, and provided a ram to sacrifice instead of the babu. The whole process involved a covenant arrangement between God and Abram. Through it all their faithfulness to each other led to the changing of Abram and Sarai's name.

Name in that context would directly imply identity, so we could say that Abraham and Sarah changed identity.

Their new names became Abraham and Sarah. The 'h' is significant because in the Hebrew it represents the word *hey* which means *empowering favor*. Their encounter with God left them better off than before.

They named their son, Isaac.

Isaac went on to have twin boys and named them Jacob and Esau. Esau was first while Jacob came out grasping his brother's heel. Later on, Jacob continued the grasping and got Esau to exchange his birthright and blessing for some of Jacob's food. After that Esau went on a murderous rampage whilst Jacob skipped town. During his journey away from the carnage, Jacob got married to two women, and found time to wrestle with an angel!

Busy guy.

Keeping with the promise made to Abraham, God found Jacob worthy and continued the covenant with Jacob. This meant changing Jacob's name. Jacob's new name became *Israel*.

Dum, dun, duh!

Most people will recognize that name!

Or country.

Fast forward many years from Jacob's change of name to a time when the Israelites came under the oppression and control of the Egyptians. It is during that time we meet Moses.

Moses assisted in the freeing of the Israelites and led them around in the desert for forty years,

twice!

These are the descendants of Abraham! There were a lot of them. The same people involved in the covenant God formed with the artist formerly known as Abram.

During their desert wandering God led and provided for his people. He guided them with a pillar of fire by night and a pillar of smoke by day. He provided food every morning too.

God was an active participant in the process of their wandering.

Those people walked and walked and walked. Other crazy things happened too! Besides the food that magically appeared every morning, Moses was able to draw water from a rock on two different occasions. One of those situations got Moses banned from the Promised Land. Doh!

At some point, the Israelites got tired of the *waiting on God for their every need part* and would complain.

They were professional complainers. Holy calf!

The Israelites desired a little bit more control concerning their circumstances.

Which would you prefer?

Slavery, hard work, and a mirage of freedom to do what you please in your spare time—hoping to not get killed by your ruler,

or

wandering around in a desert with an ever present higher being that takes care of your basic necessities….

I guess it would come down to how you look at it.

God listened to all of the complaining and finally let the people be heard. He gave them a third choice. A choice that would *in a sense* lead them back into slavery, a different kind of slavery.

God presented them with the Ten Commandments. Later on, another 600+ laws were added which can be found in the Book of Leviticus. And I thought my Lutheran catechism class was difficult.

In Exodus 19, God presented a proposal to Moses and directed him to pass along the message. Moses gather the people and gave them the new idea:

Obey a list of commands and experience *blessing* or disobey the same list and be *cursed*.

The narrative requires some inference from the reader because the people *chose* the list, God did not make them *accept* the list. What if they would have spoken up and asked, *Why a list?*

Maybe they could have said, *Well God, when you put it that way: be perfect and live or be imperfect and die—let's just keep things the way we had them before. We will stop complaining.*

God did not transcribe commands on stone with Adam, Noah, Abraham, or Jacob.

God is *relational*. To me this concept was mind-blowing. I lived to keep God happy by keeping his commands. I understood the timeline, but I did not realize the levity of the interaction between God and his people before Exodus 19. And if we want to bring up the Great Flood stuff again, my thought is this, whoever the Nephalim were, they were some bad folks and those bad folks mixed with humans and screwed up the whole lot. The flood cleared 'em out. God cares deeply about people.

Relationships need flexibility. No room for double standards. The Israelites were all about a double standard, they were given what they needed and complained about what they did not have. God gave them a chance to seemingly simplify their lives by giving them a list of obligations.

The Ten Commandments are not *bad* laws to follow.

However, it was a system based on one's performance. To keep the good times coming the Israelites had to keep God happy by *following the rules*.[1]

The solution and the problem with the law was it pointed out shortcomings. It showed us a way to live but at the same time it perfected nothing.[2]

Humankind was preoccupied with themselves.

God took care of things time and again and each time something remotely difficult presented itself, the Israelites complained and wondered why God led them out of Egypt to die.

---

[1] Exodus 19:5

[2] Hebrews 7:18

What spurs doubt and lack of faith?

A child dying?

Cancer?

Genocide?

Politics?

Those people had a flippin' pillar of fire that moved in front of them at night and it turned to smoke during the day. If the story is true then the Israelites must have been a hopeless lot because that was a daily reminder of a higher power looking over their well-being.

When times got tough the Israelites would think about themselves and what they were lacking. The law introduced a way to increase the thought of yourself. The intention of the law was to overwhelm our minds with so much narcissism, we would get sick of ourselves.

Rarely, do I finish a whole *stack of* pancakes. Most of the time, whenever I crave pancakes I eat half of them and wonder, *why am I still eating pancakes?*

I get that way whenever I try to please God. I eventually fail and wonder, *why am I still trying to make God happy with me?*

The law was meant to bring me to the end of well,

me.

Upon that arrival, I see God was there the whole time. The law shows me how I am not God. If I let God be God then whenever tough times come, God is always there to pick up the pieces. Now, I am learning God not only picks up those pieces, but he teaches me how to think and make decisions like him.

Instead, as a young Christian, I was taught to memorize the law.

To be a *good* Christian, I had to *avoid* sin.

The battle between grace and sin raged in my heart. I was always thinking about sin.

Is this a sin?

Was that a sin?

"God, forgive me for the sins I am not aware that I committed today,[3] I don't want to go to hell."

God is something else if after admitting I am imperfect and *not God,* I would still have to seek forgiveness for things I do in ignorance.

Thank goodness the Bible says God is love[4] and this is why God found fault with this covenant based on a law.[5]

So we eliminate the pride that can accompany our ability to follow the law. For if we are conscious of sin then we are not conscious of God.[6]

Confess your sin, Nolan! Grace only covers what you confess. (Yikes)

It is not that truth is a matter of perspective so much as my perspective affects how I interpret truth.

Studies have found that hearing and vision impairments negatively impact learning in that it changes the standard by which someone is graded.[7]

It's science.

---

[3] Hebrews 9:7

[4] 1 John 4:8

[5] Hebrews 8:7-13

[6] Hebrews 10:2-3

[7] Virginia E. Bishop, Ph.D.. *Preschool Children with Visual Impairments.* 1996. http://www.tsbvi.edu/instructional-resources/1069-preschool-children-with-visual-impairments-by-virginia-bishop

Someone who is mute can learn at the same rate as someone who can talk and both people have sound hearing and vision. Even with tools like Braille and visual aids, it takes the average person a little bit longer to understand the lesson.[8]

I can *see* just like the Israelites could see the works of God.

However, due to their preoccupation with themselves they lacked perspective negatively impacting their perception of God.

For years, I was shackled by a misperception of the law.

The law says do not sin or you will die.
Grace says if you sin grace covers all that you do.

The law says, do not commit adultery.
Grace asks: why are you committing adultery? What's the benefit?

The law states don't do this or don't do that.
Grace expresses, how will your life be affected by this action, are you being the person you were created to be?

The law draws out sin. Points out your wrongdoing.
Grace frees us from our sin. Encourages us by saying "You are not perfect, do not let the pursuit discourage you!"

The law serves as a limited guide by which to live.
Grace fulfills the law so that we do not have to.

The law limits what we can do by showing us our shortcomings.
Grace diverts God's eyes from our shortcomings by fixing them on Jesus the ultimate sacrifice and the perfecter of our faith.

The law destroys.
Grace gives life.

---

[8] Reed, Maureen; Curtis, Kathryn. "Experiences of Students with Visual Impairments in Canadian Higher Education." *Journal of Visual Impairment & Blindness*, Vol. 106, No. 7, July 2012. https://www.questia.com/library/journal/1G1-298056830/experiences-of-students-with-visual-impairments-in

We turn from sin not because God commands us to do so, but it is to our benefit to remember God.

Sure, I agree that to *fear* God is the beginning of all wisdom, but we hold the paradoxical thought that God is beyond our comprehension so as to induce fear yet, God is not angry and tells the world that *perfect love casts out fear.*

Focusing on God requires that we focus less on other things.

To hang out with your family or friends you need to sacrifice other things.

Let me give an example. I like to play poker.

Gambling is not a sin because I am a bad steward with my money. Gambling is an emptying work by which it steals time from my family to gamble. When I lose, I lose money that could have been used elsewhere. Gambling is not a sin per se, but are there areas in my life that could benefit from the money I gambled away?

But Nolan, I don't lose.

Fair enough, this is why perspective matters. Why am I gambling? I call it entertainment. It is cheaper than attending a ball game or going to the movies. I don't wager much. Poker is time spent with friends.

What if I upped the ante and start gambling away my paycheck?

What if I start maxing out my credit cards to support this *entertainment?*

What if the entertainment becomes a *habit*?

If I did that, when would I think of God?

When I wanted to win? When I needed an Ace on the river?

How full would I feel after losing thousands of dollars on gambling?

How about excessive drinking?
Doing drugs?
Lying?

Being apathetic...
Watching porn...
Masturbating.
Cutting yourself...
Hours in front of the television/phone/computer...
Intellectual pursuit…
Worrying…

A few of these are 'sins' but most of them are taxing my hope in life.

We walk around questioning our purpose yet we fill our time with nonsense. It's not about *sin* it's about our *focus*.

Grace frees my focus to see and experience God.

Different people kick various habits due to various reasons. This next sentence is strictly for Christians. *In modern Christianity, many people are concerned more with their freedoms than they are on the one who issued said freedom.*

What about the person who does not adhere to a higher power,

is there still sin?

Of course.

Anyone would agree they are *imperfect*.

The good news is God's only requirement for an abundant and eternal life is *perfection*.

Wait, good news?

Yup. Looking at God in this way completely altered my understanding.

To be with God we start with the Christ Jesus. Jesus explained no one gets to the Father except through him.

The Ten Commandments were a foreshadow of what life should look like.

Re-read the list.

If this almighty God exists then the list would make sense. The list is a decent guide.

We get to God through Christ not because Jesus is bouncing the door to the VIP section of heaven but because we have *faith* that his birth, life, death, and resurrection happened and had purpose!

Faith that it actually happened.

Faith that it was backed by God's declaration of *I made all of you and desire reconciliation*. Or, "Let's be friends."

This ministry of grace and reconciliation is what allows me to participate in a friendship with God. When God looks at me he no longer sees my sin, he sees Jesus and Jesus is perfect.

This is why we initially confess of our *sin or our lack of perfection*.

'Initially' is the operative word. We confess our sin once because our confession becomes one of *faith*.

When I confessed I was a sinner, Jesus responded by saying, "I know, I got this" and pointed me toward God. I cried out for answers and because God saw Jesus, he heard my prayer and answered.[9]

He invested in me, so I invest in him.

I confess *faith* and repent of *sin*.

Another way of saying this is *we talk of Jesus and change our minds about how we live our life*.

How similar are my closest relationships with people here on earth. Do they represent in any way the friendship I have with God?

Do we move around in friendship with people by worrying whether or not we

---

[9] Prayer is a big deal. I wish I spent more time discussing it, but *prayer* is a loaded term and it was not something of a struggle for me. I thoroughly enjoy my conversations with the Father.

have sinned against them by the things we do or do we think of things to do with our friends?

We think of our friend's interests.

We talk about life.

We share the good and bad times with those people.

If that is earthly, limited, and imperfect friendship, how much better is friendship with the one who created us?

God is someone who chooses not to see our shortcomings. He is someone that only seeks our relationship. And because we relate with him our lives are full and whole!

God didn't create us to mindlessly worship him. He created us to have real relationship. One that has two parties giving 100% of each other for the betterment of the other!

God may convict and discipline, but show me one person who doesn't seek to succeed at something by learning the disciplines of the task!

God is not a taskmaster or an accuser. He is a father who wants to grow us, spend time with us, and remind us on a daily basis he is glad to be our friend.

I cannot reconcile the things God did in the Old Testament. Thankfully, that is not my job. However, my limited understanding would suggest that God is passionate for his creation, but creation kept rejecting him time and again. I don't know for sure, but that is one thought.

Maybe I jumped the gun, but now is as good time as any to talk about Jesus.

Chapter 8:
Jesus Superstar!

Who is Jesus?

I mean really, who is he?

To start, *Jesus* really is not his name. Back to the whole translation thing. The origin of Jesus' name goes back thousands of years.

What's in a name?

We get *Jesus* from Latin, which came from the Greek. Its Hebrew origin is similar to the name we translate as *Joshua* in the Old Testament.

The name means *deliverer.*

Wait, was Jesus real?

Once, I watched a documentary where all of these notable scholars, some of them atheists discuss the reality of a *historical Jesus*. That is fancy talk for *Jesus was a real person who walked the earth.* Google: *Historicity of Jesus.*

There is plenty of historical evidence to suggest that Abraham Lincoln was a real person. It is kind of hard to fabricate a president, but for you and me, we did not get the opportunity to talk with Mr. Lincoln and see for ourselves that he existed.

Not all famous historical figures/events like Alexander the Great, King Tut, Napoleon Bonaparte, Trojan War, or the 300 Spartans, have the amount of documentation to back up their stories. The information is quite minimal compared to other things described in history. Furthermore, history is written by the winners. Some winners like to sensationalize things.

For our understanding of Jesus we have his legacy, which has spanned over 2000 years. Pretty good for a guy who died a death culturally equivalent to the modern day electric chair. The description of Jesus in the Bible has been painted, literally and figuratively, in so many scenes, lights, and backgrounds that it is hard to wade through the murky waters that is the identity of Christ Jesus, the *Son of God*.

I heard someone say that either Jesus was insane or he was right. That is kind of bold, especially if you are looking for a middle ground when it comes to Truth. It is hard to ignore the topic of Jesus. There are plenty of Bible thumpers who will make sure to stand up on your corner and preach Jesus!

Jesus is not going away. I will mark that up as a win.

Really though, who was he?

More respectively, who *is* he?

Why would anyone believe anything I would have to say on the subject?

Well, I am a *seed planter*.

Sure, I have a couple letters after my name. Although, they are few in comparison to the amount of letters after the name of my mentor from graduate school, but I have enough to make my mother care.

The Bible says a lot, and this is not a textbook, so I will be brief.

In short, Jesus is God.

See Christians do not believe in multiple gods. That is something unique about Judaism and Christianity, they are monotheists.

One god or God.[10]

There are other beliefs with a similar view, but whenever the Bible was written, there were many people groups who followed after multiple gods or identified many gods as a way to explain their existence (i.e. Ancient Egyptians & Greeks).

---

[10] In case you were wondering, some Christians like to capitalize stuff pertaining to anything Holy. Nothing wrong with it, but wanted to let you know.

So to say that Jesus is God can be a little confusing. If God is God, and Jesus was a man, furthermore, Jesus is the SON of God, and we cannot forget about the Holy Spirit, how is it, where do I, what the f*%$?

If every part of Christianity could be explained logically with a 100% comprehension rate, then there would not be much room for faith. Furthermore, saying faith is a requirement is not a cop-out, but a reiteration, as everything in life requires a *little* faith.

The Bible was written by many people over the course of a thousand something years. They used the resources and words available to them to accurately communicate whatever truth God wanted them to write. One of those situations in the New Testament involved Jesus and others talking about how Jesus is the *Son* of God. Nowhere does it say that Jesus *is* God, per se.

There is a whole Church doctrine on this thing called: *The Trinity*. It implies in some crude way, of which there is no real metaphor to use, the Trinity is God, Jesus, and the Holy Spirit. They are not three separate deities, but one deity in three parts, but one deity with no real distinguishable definition because they are three, but one. There's three, but really, it's God divided but not really, because God is one.

I hope that cleared things up. I hope you enjoyed the book. Tell your friends.

…

Still here? Great. I am not getting out of this that easily.

Son in the Greek culture meant *of the same flesh*.[11]

I am Nolan son of Bruce of the Recker clan. Because Bruce and I share the same blood, we are one, of the same flesh. That is why the Bible also uses the metaphor in marriage that the man and woman will leave their families and then join to each other and become *one flesh*.

---

[11] The Greek word is huios pronounced hwee-os. It often means "one who shares a special relationship with or a likeness to someone or something."

Let me make things more confusing. The Bible gives us all these names to describe Jesus. The Bible is big on names, by the way. Better than a phone book, I promise. One of the names used to describe Jesus is *Immanuel*, which means, *God with us*.

To recap, Jesus means *deliverer,* is of *one flesh* with God, and is also *God with us*.

Jesus is God.

No getting around it. God, in order to fulfill humankind's, specifically Israel's, portion of the covenant had to become fully human and live a perfect life on earth. Free of sin.

At the same time, though, Jesus is *man.* He was born of a woman, a virgin woman.

Jesus always referred to himself as the *Son of Man*. This is another paradox. Jesus is the Son of Man *and* the Son of God.

So, God came to earth as a human, lived as a human and died as a human. Then he rose from the dead.

This concept was tough for me to comprehend, was Jesus, God? Or was Jesus a man? Was he both? Did he go back and forth? Was he confused?

This is important to Christianity because, it matters.

Some people find it hard to swallow that Jesus was fully a man. More people find it harder to swallow that Jesus was and is God.

Concerning his humanity and alleged deity-status, Jesus had to spend time with the Father. So, Jesus *is* God, but he had to spend time *with* God? This causes many issues.

This is one *chapter* on Jesus. I have read many *books* about Jesus. There is not enough space here, but I will say a couple more things regarding Jesus as a man and Jesus as God.

There is a recurring story in the first three books of the New Testament about a woman who for twelve years suffered from ceaseless bleeding.[12]

In this story with the woman, it is said that Jesus was on his way to see a twelve-year-old girl who was dying.

In the Middle East, public areas and marketplaces are so full of people it is nearly impossible to not to bump into someone. On this particular day, the people were shoulder to shoulder, people were pressing in on all sides. The story goes that as Jesus was on his way to see this twelve-year-old girl, a woman pushed through the crowd, reached out and touched Jesus.

Instantly, the woman was healed of her infirmity.

The Bible says that he felt "power leave [him]." Jesus *felt* it.

Jesus stopped, and the disciples as usual were confused asking, "Jesus, what is it?"
"Someone touched me!"

The disciples tried to hold back their laughter, "Uh, Jesus, buddy, we are all being touched, some of us in ways we have never been touched before." Thomas snickered as a not as cool disciple elbowed him.

The first part is a paraphrase, "First Thomas, that's inappropriate, second, are you doubting me?"

Thomas was offended, "No! Never!"

"Thomas, that is what we call a double negative, no wonder you failed out of rabbinic school." Jesus turns his focus to the rest of the disciples, "This was something different, power went out of me."

The angels and some others are up in heaven ad-libbing like a bad lip-sync video on YouTube.

Gabriel, imitating Peter, "Are you sure you didn't pass gas or something, Jesus?"

---

[12] Mark 5:21-43, Matthew 9:18-26, Luke 8:40-56

Michael, speaking as John, "Peter, you wanker, Jesus didn't have any of those wretched beans you cooked us for lunch."

Moses, speaking as Matthew, "This is all really taxing, dontchya think?"

The disciples tried reasoning with Jesus that they could not possibly find who or what touched Jesus as there were so many people. The woman realized she caused a situation, revealed herself, and then explained the "whole truth."[13]

Did Jesus know who it was that touched him?

Does it matter?

To some, it does and here is why. If Jesus was drinking his God-go-go juice then Jesus knows everything. If that is true, then he knew who touched him.

To others, if Jesus was rocking the man-suit, then as a man, he does not know everything and so must rely on God for complete direction. Jesus asks who touched him because he genuinely did not know.

Which one is true?

Does it matter?

If Jesus is God then we can say Jesus had the *ability* to know everything, but often chose to operate within the limitations of his humanity.

Either way, Jesus fulfilled the Old Testament covenant. Jesus still went on to prove himself to be practically perfect in every way.

The aforementioned story in light of Jesus' fulfillment of covenant does not seem to matter.

Unless, it does matter. Then in that case, which one is it? Perhaps, a spoonful of sugar will help?

---

[13] Mark 5:33

Jesus is the typical Sunday School answer. Regardless of where anyone stands in relation to their belief in God, most people will agree that Jesus was

a fantastic teacher,

person,

philanthropist,

man, etc.

Jesus was both 100% God and 100% Man. Paradox.

Jesus knew the entire law because he memorized it. At the same time, he was not on the God-go-go juice and dealt with all the same temptations men and women deal with.

It can be argued, Jesus could not use his deity to side-step sin. He had to face it head on as a human. The law has rules. God cannot cheat the system.

Paradox.

It is a matter of perspective. From one side, it looks one way, from the other, it appears differently.

The Bible says love is defined by laying down your life for another.[14] In the grandest gesture of affection God put the desires of man before His own. In order for man to again have the opportunity for an unadulterated relationship with whatever they want, the law had to be dealt with. God became human and showed the world who he was.

Jesus once said, "If you have seen me, then you have seen the one who sent me."[15]

For us, we can read, "What you read of what I said and did, those are the words and actions of the one who sent me."

---

[14] 1 John 3:16

[15] John 14:7-9

It's crazy, of all the signs and miracles that Jesus performed, many people struggled to take hold of or jump on the Jesus bandwagon. However, many did. The ones who opted out of following Jesus were the ones who thought they had all of the answers. I don't have all of the answers. I have some! Well, I think I do anyway, but I am always open to correction and direction.

There were some people at the time of Jesus who thought they knew everything about God. Their knowledge puffed them up and they acted as mediators between those who lacked knowledge of the Scriptures and God.

It is a little bit different today. Anybody with a computer, Internet access, and who has a semi-intelligible thought can post something for the world to read. Back then people relied heavily on the religious leaders for guidance. In a way, it still happens, but the requirements seem to matter less and less when it comes to sharing an opinion.

Man wanted real freedom; freedom from obligation.

Obligation is slavery. Think about it.

Love, is not obligation.

Somewhere along the way, *love* lost its meaning.

Love is sacrifice.

Obligation involves sacrifice, but it is almost involuntary. When it comes to obligation, you get stuck between a rock and a hard place.

God was not obligated to man.

God loves man.

Jesus is the white flag.

Not the white flag of surrender, but the white flag of peace.

Jesus is God showing the world that God has not forgotten the world. In a way, God was obligated to the law. That is why he sent Jesus!

God loved the world, so he laid down his life. However, God was obligated to the law and knew it was still relevant as long as it was never fulfilled. God put on the jersey of the other team and showed love, by dying.

The Apostle Paul talks about this grand gesture as *God's ministry of reconciliation*. That God, through the faithfulness of Jesus: Jesus' sacrifice and his rising from the dead; rose the white flag and negotiated new terms.

Jesus fulfilled the law by keeping every letter of it. All man has to do is believe that Jesus died and rose again. Instead of obligation to the law, man is free to love God. We view God through the words and actions of Jesus. Those things show us who God is.

In turn, God views us through the sacrifice of Jesus. Because of Jesus, God chooses to focus on the finished product. God looks at our finished product in Jesus who teaches us how to be mature and complete.

One of the ways we learn to be like God is to look at Jesus.

The law points out things in ourselves. It shows where we are lacking. The law turns our focus on ourselves.

Jesus freed us from that.

God is not puffed up by his knowledge and strength, lording over us and watching us scurry around, judging others in comparison to our strengths and abilities.

If love is laying down your life for another, then God showed us that all of this, everything in the universe is not about Him. More so, it is about God's love.

It is not about God, but we have to look to him to learn from him.

Paradox.

Understanding any of this is based on what we believe or what we decide to put our faith in.

Chapter 9:
Faith, Simply

"I have learned that faith means trusting in advance what will only make sense in reverse." - Philip Yancey

Jesus said that "My yoke is easy and my burden is light." He is not talking about eggs. If it was about eggs then sign me up because I appreciate all parts of the egg: good and bad cholesterol. Sadly, *yoke* means the wooden thing slung over the back of steers/cows/camels/horses as they pull whatever it is they are told to pull.

It may just be me, but I neglect to think this yoke is easy. Often, I am surrounded by people that melodramatize a lot of things about the Christian *faith*. These things include, but are not limited to God's wrath, sin, the Devil, salvation, and prosperity Gospel people.

Christianity can be downright confusing as hell. Oh wait.

There are so many of us running around or in some cases sitting still and typing away on a keyboard about their opinion on this or that in Christianity. When some of us encounter someone that disagrees with our point of view, how often do we kindly discuss our disagreements? I see much judgment and exclusion in the Church. The Church is made up of Christians, so I can see it is hard for many to reconcile Jesus' easy yoke and light burden.

It is ugly.

Having faith can be ugly.

I grew up in church and was almost as equally as confused! I wish faith had been explained to me in terms that *made sense.*

The English word—*faith* is used a bunch to translate a couple different words in the New Testament. You read that right. We got stuck with most English translations using one English word to translate multiple Greek words. Oh Bill Shakespeare! To be, or not to be, that is the…never mind.

My understanding of *faith* had more to do with a metaphorical power bar. Reminds me of the turbo button in a video game. You go faster for a time, but eventually the bar runs out and you need to lay off of it until it reloads. The following phrases have been touted and paraded during sermons on faith.

"Faith the size of a mustard seed…"

"A faith that can move mountains."

"Just have faith…"

The last one reminds me of the former Nike brand slogan: "Just do it."

I wonder if there has been a youth pastor somewhere who used that line once or twice in response to a difficult "Why" question by one of their students.

High School Student (Inquisition): "Why?"

Pastor: "Just do it."

High School Inquisition: "You just repeated what my shirt reads. Explain to me the 'why' concerning this difficult theological topic! And don't give me a politically correct answer to appease the Elders so they don't fire you for *rocking the boat.*"

Pastor: "Just about that time for youth group to be over. See you next week for the pie eating contest and we will talk about nominally conservative subjects that are easy to explain and can be cut with a theological cookie cutter of which will not prepare most of you for college causing most of you to rethink your faith and leave the church for a decade or so."

High School Inquisition: "Yay! Pie!"

It is a tough business, Christianity. For those of us that align with Christianity, that is a deadly statement. Christianity being a business. We do not want to confuse that with a large chain of Christian owned arts and crafts stores. Or anything else that identifies itself as explicitly Christian, i.e. music, movies, paintings, books, etc.

Christianity is one of those things that offers an explanation for all of existence. Pieces of which we have already explored. A fancy word for this explanation is *metanarrative*. It is a large overarching story of which all other smaller stories or truths fall under the metaphorical umbrella of *metanarrative*. The thing about Christianity as a metanarrative, is it requires a certain confidence, belief, or faith by anyone who adheres to the *story*.

This is not a foreign topic to anyone. Muslims, scientists, atheists, my wife handing me the grocery shopping list, etc. all require a certain level of faith in whatever truth they hold to. Does the *story* possess the necessary answers to appease the one who is practicing *faith?*

Muslims believe in Allah.

Scientists believe in empirical evidence.

Atheists believe there are no gods or God. Their *faith* lies within *self.*

This is quote is from the atheists.org/about-us page:

"An atheist loves himself and his fellow man instead of a god. An atheist accepts that heaven is something for which we should work now – here on earth – for all men together to enjoy. An atheist accepts that he can get no help through prayer, but that he must find in himself the inner conviction and strength to meet life, to grapple with it, to subdue it and to enjoy it. An atheist accepts that only with a knowledge of himself and a knowledge of his fellow man can he find the understanding that will help lead to a life of fulfillment."

One thing Christians and Atheists can agree on is this:

"An atheist accepts that heaven is something for which we should work now – here on earth – for all men together to enjoy."

Heaven is a Christian topic. One of the things Jesus teaches on prayer is to say, "On earth as it is in heaven."

I will not address *end times* theories in this book, but Christ gave a couple mandates about spreading the love of God *on* earth.

Believing God is love requires faith.

When I go to the grocery store, my wife believes I am only going to get the things on the grocery list and not anything else my sweet tooth may desire that I will consume on the drive home.

Christianity requires faith.

This is where I got confused. I hope the following clarification of faith comes in handy. I heard multiple explanations of faith, but rarely one as concise as Mr. Yancey's understanding of *faith*.

There is a cool scene in the movie Seven Days in Utopia where Robert Duvall's character explains to Lucas Black's character that the game of golf is always played in *front* of the ball.

However, before the described moment Black's character played golf thinking about previous shots, not once focusing on what lies ahead. Instead, he would think about the anger, disappointments, his form, lie of the ball, bad weather, etc.

It is fiction, but the story was written by a Sports Psychologist who just so happens to adhere to the Christian faith. I think there is truth in the metaphor and it directly points to a clear understanding of *faith.*

To me, faith became a solution, not a process.

In times of doubt, I would be directed to have faith. If the future seemed uncertain, I was to have faith that everything would work itself out the way God wanted it to happen. In a way faith recognizes *God is in control.* I do not doubt God's ability, but I may take precedent with his decisions. He and I don't always agree.

Some people believe that God controls everything. That is his thing. He works for the good of those who love him and at times, he allows certain things to happen as part of some great scheme to one day show the world the true magnitude of his glory.

I think that puts God in a box. It classifies God as someone who lacks faith. If he cannot give some type of control or choice to his creation, then God has no faith at all, and so cultivates a double standard by controlling everything and requiring his constituents to exhibit something God chooses not to practice.

God has the knowledge, power, and frequent flyer miles to manipulate whatever he wants to whenever he wants to. However, I think God acts within a limited system. He chooses to operate within the ebb and flow of *relationship*.

God chooses to pursue humankind. God is faithful when we are not.

We all have the freedom to choose God. If God controls everything, then do we really have free will? Some folks would say *no*.

God is an infinite idea.

This discussion toes the line of thought: which came first the egg or the chicken?

If the unlimited or infinite did not exist before man, how would man conceive something that reached beyond the limits of death? Here is another way of explaining it. Picture yourself without a nose. After you get the picture of Lord Voldemort out of your brain, think of yourself. What do you look like? Is it odd?

What if nobody in the entire world ever had a nose? If we never knew an existence with a nose, then would it be weird for someone to see someone without a nose? There is no opposite with which to compare. Same thing with the infinite and the finite. This is not concrete logic, but nonetheless a logical progression in its own right. Which came first, the finite or the infinite?

Maybe the infinite is a man-made thing?

Is the previous question unanswerable like the following question?

How many licks does it take to get to the center of a Tootsie Pop?

Faith is a loaded concept.

The way faith was painted for me as a child and well into college was simple and measurable. You either have it, or you don't, and others could see how much faith you had based on the life you lived.

Faith became a product.

When in doubt, I would pop some faith into the toaster and bam, the product would pop up ready for some butter. If things did not go my way in a certain situation where I had *faith*, I would check the toaster for errors. Let's assume the toaster represents God.[16]

I put my toast *in* God. Wait…

In Western culture, the capitalist idea is when I invest, I am to expect a return on my investment.

Let me neglect the lack of relationship I may have with God before the situation arose that required a little faith, but my expectation is whenever needed, pop some faith into the toaster and bam, the product pops up and after I add the butter, sprinkle on some cinnamon and sugar. Life is sweet.

At some point along the way someone explained faith is a *means* not a solution or a product.

This led me to ask, "What is the median and the mode? Should I do the average too? Wait, mean is another way of saying average? Ah forget it, I'm gonna make some toast."

Faith as a means to an end scratches at the surface of what faith is, but still points toward a proverbial retirement plan like a 401k. God will match up to 3% of whatever I deposit from my faith-check. Investing is a means. Faith becomes my solution for retirement. In the world of employment, you put aside part of your earnings so that once you turn sixty-five-ish you will have money and you can retire. Rarely would you get to touch the money before it's time. Unfortunately, many Christians have reduced faith to a similar concept. Faith makes you rich (The Bible would say righteous) qualifying you for heaven. Faith is the investment for whenever you retire from life and fly away to your mansion in the sky.

Faith is not a product.

Faith is a process.

---

[16] A microwave could work too. Or genie lamp. Same line of thought: quick fix.

Faith is not always simple.

Where does faith, *begin*?

As complex as faith can be, I think it starts with gratitude.

Faith points outward much like gratitude points toward a giver.

I thank God for his faithfulness and pursuit of me.

Simple, right? Let's get complicated.

The go-to verse for defining faith is "the reality of what is hoped for, the proof of what is not seen" (Hebrews 11:1). In a way, as of the writing of this book, I have faith that the front office of the Chicago Cubs are building a solid farm system of young players who will grow to play their way toward winning the World Series. Call me, crazy.

Thank you, I have been called worse.

On an insignificant level, the hope of the Cubs winning the World Series sits on the assumption that the Cubs will one day win the World Series. At this time, it has been over 100 years since the last time the Cubs won it all. However, this example may not resonate with everyone. Faith for you, me, homeless guy in the inner-city, a widow in Africa, or a refugee in the Middle East will all have its own identity, but the mutual understanding is the same.

Faith is *belief*.

The two transliterated Greek New Testament words from which we get faith are *pistis* and *pistuo*.

Pistis has various understandings based on the context in which it is used. Some of those meanings are, "what can be believed," "faith of," "faithfulness of," or "trustworthiness."

Some interesting things about this word: It is used most by the Apostle Paul reflecting about Jesus and someone's response to Jesus. The two books where the word is found the most are Romans and Hebrews.

Pistuo also has various understandings based on the context in which it is used. Some of those meanings are, "what can be believed," "to be entrusted with," or "confidence in." An interesting thing about this word is that it is most used in the first four books of the New Testament: Matthew, Mark, Luke, and John.

Matthew and the boys are considered *gospels*. Gospel is a fancy word for *good news*. The idea being that these works are the ESPN: Top Plays of Jesus of Nazareth.

It lays the framework for who Jesus was and is. It is not a coincidence then that *pistuo* is used most in the four gospels as Jesus spoke much of who he was and his purpose. The importance being Jesus was telling the truth or he was a raving lunatic who fooled a bunch of people.

Some would say faith in Jesus was just as important then as it is, today. Furthermore, Jesus *entrusted* many teachings to the disciples and trained them in telling others about the truth.

The word *pistis* is used in these four books, but not as often. The coincidence of its frequency in Romans and Hebrews is interesting because those two books are the infrastructure of Jesus. The gospels were the framework and the foundation, and the writers of Romans and Hebrews gives more detail to the framework that Jesus built they are the guts and the insides. The focus being that God is faithful to us, as Jesus was faithful to God, so we too are to be faithful to God.

Jesus consistently presented that anything he taught had to be *believed*. The Apostle John quoted Jesus using the word *pistuo,* eighty-five times. If you dared it, you could accuse Jesus of trying too hard. Only problem is Jesus backed up all the *"believe me"* lingo with miracles. Jesus was like a magician who showed you how to do his tricks except that he was not peddling tricks.

He was personifying a new way of living.

The Apostle Paul did not have to improve off of what Jesus taught, instead Paul expanded on it. Jesus did not explicitly say a lot of things. I think Jesus did this on purpose. Even so, Jesus even said a couple times in so many words, "If you don't believe what I said, in the very least believe what I did, rest assured that one of those two things are true."

Jesus came as the manifested word of God, showing the world that God was no longer angry, he was calling a truce and led by example the life he wishes for all those that believe it to be true.

Compare this new life to a new car.[17] Imagine Jesus shows up at your house and says to you, "Here is a brand new car, fully-loaded, and it is all yours. Here are the keys, if you believe I have already paid for it, then you can have it. Free of charge. If you think it is stolen or that you have to pay me back, then leave it here. At least take the keys, it is yours whenever you want it. By the way, On-Star, GPS Navigation, and Sirius-XM Radio are also provided. Twenty-four hours a day, seven days a week, 365 days a year, direct connect to the Big Man Upstairs. If you have any questions, see the owner's manual, if you are still confused, we are always available."

In a way, The Apostle Paul is *Customer Support*.

Paul had an interaction with Jesus except it was not as pleasant as receiving a new car, er camel. It was an intense game of hide-and-go-seek. Something blinded Paul. Jesus spoke to Paul and instructed him to find someone. Jesus handed the *keys* to the guy Paul had to find (Acts 9).

Paul also translated for different people groups and backgrounds. In the time period that Paul lived, he mediated between the news of the car, the Jews' understanding of camels and donkeys, and everyone else who used chariots. Paul traveled all over the country explaining the new car, its benefits, and how people could receive theirs. He highlighted what features were available. He addressed the unlimited possibilities with the car and how you have to use your imagination to fully utilize it. He also stressed that in order to fully appreciate the new car, you had to quit driving or riding your old camel, donkey, horse, or chariot.

Faith or belief frees us to enjoy this new car. As with any car, one has to maintain it. The new car runs on software that never requires updating, but it does require user interaction and acknowledgments. With each interaction, your understanding of the car's capabilities grows, your gratitude increases, and the performance of the vehicle is more recognized.

---

[17] I am borrowing the car metaphor from Graham Cooke's teaching series, *Mind of a Saint*.

Everyone gets the same car, but not everyone works through the interactive software the same way as everyone else. Some will need to learn what the car can do in a mountainous terrain. Others will need to take it through a desert. And others will need to test how it floats or flies. Each person gets the opportunity to utilize their car to travel where they never dreamt could be possible.

That is faith.

It is interacting with the giver. The car will only take you as far as you will let it go.

I always understood the opposite. Faith meant surviving when in all actuality *faith is meant for thriving.*

Thriving is a process. Everyday I learn what God has in store for me. I believe that because of Jesus, God sees who I can become. By believing in Jesus, I acknowledge there is a difference between him and me, and that Jesus is the better option. Believing in Jesus grants me direct access to God. My faith says, "I want to be like Jesus." God acknowledges that and says, "O.k., I will teach you."

To some it comes easy. To some, it comes like Paul's experience and is extremely difficult. Faith is not easy, but it does not have to be extremely difficult.

Or, maybe faith is extremely difficult, but what about the yoke and burden and all of that?

If you are anything like me, I did not like the idea of *faith*. To me, there was no joy in it. Life was hard. Faith did not teach me a thing. All along, God was *trying* to teach me something through my faith, but I was only taught to endure and *let God handle it*.

God was trying to teach me how to handle things. Faith is to be enjoyed. The Bible says that God's strength is made perfect in our weakness. It is not that God wants me walking around all mopey-like wallowing in my weaknesses. When a weakness is identified in me,

faith says God is at work in my life teaching me something new about himself.

God shows me how he would handle it. This transcends age, culture, and economic status. God is the God of everyone. And in each unique situation, God desires to teach his creation how he would do it.

We approach faith in joy. There has to be joy in the process of learning about God. It directly influences our immediate circumstances. The lessons may be easy or hard, but in each challenge, there is an opportunity to practice what God would do, or fail and get the opportunity to try again and again until we get it. God is gracious like that.[18] He wants the most for us.

I learned it comes down to my faith to determine if I want to interact and learn something new…

or not.

---

[18] This example can also be found in the above teaching series by Graham Cooke.

<u>Chapter 10:</u>
Love Bug, It Stinks!
Wait, It's A Stink Bug!

Love.

Just do it.

I flirted with the writing of this chapter like the twelve-year-old version of me flirted with Trina, the thirteen-year-old girl at our school car wash fundraiser. We were *going steady* and I wanted to *leave my mark* like one who gives away their class ring or letterman jacket.

What's a letterman jacket, Nolan?

For the generationally gapped, I wanted us to be *Facebook Official* before there was Facebook.

I remember that we had not yet kissed, on the lips, (I just pictured the seven year old version of me giggling) so as far as letting people know, *Hey, she's mine*. I decided to mix it up. I took my wet hands and firmly placed them on her shirt,

right on her back.

Seriously, it was her back like a child marking wet concrete. I put my hands on her back to get her shirt wet. Maybe people would ask, "*Those are some beautiful handprints on your shirt, to whom do they belong?*"

She laughed and acted annoyed. Not a single person asked about the handprints. They quickly dried or got covered up, as the rest of the shirt got wet. However, the relationship changed as her plan to get into a relationship with a younger boy to make another guy jealous paid off when not more than two weeks after that moment she broke up with me as the boy she really wanted, in his jealousy, asked her out.

I think I cried.

I mean, I toughened up and acted like a man spouting shenanigans like, "I got ninety-nine problems, but a [girl] ain't one!"

Seriously, though. I cried like a boy who had witnessed his parents get divorced, gone to live with his evil step-mother and returned home; hopeful that one day in his short existential wanderings he will find a woman who will love him forever. I was a poor sap.

This is a *chapter* on love.

There are *books* written on the subject.

This is not an attempt to fall in line with Westernized reductionist reasoning and take a topic prone to wide interpretation and experiences and reduce it to a couple well written remarks sprinkled with some personal stories.

Nevertheless, Jesus summed up the entire Old Testament law with the command, "Love one another" (John 13:34-35) I am not Jesus, but do not be surprised if we arrive at the same conclusion.

What I did not know about love through the lens of Christianity is that, in the Bible, wherever we read the word, *love*, lies behind it one of four or so Hebrew words in the Old Testament and four words in the New Testament. I want to briefly touch on each word from the New Testament and mention another Greek word used for love that is not in the Bible, but is the root for a popular English word.

A reminder, the goal of this book was not to piece together a *new theology*, but express things I learned after twenty years of dancing with Christianity and hopefully present my shift in perspective toward an unified effort of like-minded conversation about the Christian faith and move forward with an intentional call to band together under the banner that is *God's grace*.

"For God so *loved* the world…" Give yourself five points if you finished the rest of that verse in your head. Give yourself seven points if you said it out loud.

The root word for this type of love is transliterated, *agape*.

This is the Godzilla of all understandings of love. It is destructive to *self*.

"Love looks not to its own interests."

Agape by definition is to lay one's life down for another. So love in that sense is to put someone else before yourself. This is not an "if it is convenient, I will consider someone else's feelings before my own." Agape is a complete abandoning of self-preservation.

If self-centeredness was Tokyo, then Godzilla is love.

The second word used in the New Testament for love is *phileo*. You may have heard of the famous or is it infamous, city in Philadelphia known as the city of *brotherly love*?

Its construction is from two Greek words, *phileo* and *adelphos*. Phileo means "to love" and adelphos means "brother." Phileo in the simplest sense is to love someone on the level of friend or peer. Today, *love* has become as versatile in the English language as the *F-word*.

Another Greek word found in the New Testament that is not translated as love, but has a similar connotation is, *schploknan*. Commonly, it is translated as *compassion*. It means to *spill out your entrails*. That is a fancy way to say *intestines*. It takes place whenever we encounter a situation that requires significant attention and care, which is confirmed by a stirring in our stomach. Some people also call that your *gut-feeling* or your *second-brain*.[19]

The same idea applies, it is a response to someone or something outside of yourself regardless of the personal implications.

The fourth Greek word used only one time in the book of Romans and explained in great detail by C.S. Lewis in his work *The Four Loves,* is the word *philostorge*. You may have guessed it, but it is the combination of *phileo* and another word. That word is *storge*. This word is translated as *affection* or familial love. It is the natural attention you show to those with whom you share a special connection.

The fifth Greek word that I would like to involve in this short little diddy on *love* is the word *eros*. This word is the inspiration for *erotic-love*, often the focus of desire, passion, or lust. It is kind of unfair to lump that word in as the springboard for lust because lust gets a bad rap in the Bible.

---

[19] Michael D. Gershon, M.D. *The Second Brain.* 1998. Pages xi-xvi.

I am not defending lust in the *sinful* sense. Here I go, getting all defensive and such. I will continue on.

Eros gets a better explanation by the ancient philosopher Plato when he explains in his Symposium dialogues that eros is the vision/focus/appreciation one person has for the inner beauty of another.

Its transition to passion is a natural occurrence in the sense that one person sees or feels something in relation to the person in question that is deeper than the surface. A passionate arousal drawing that person like a bug into the light.

Zap.

Are you still with me?

Love is,

complicated.

Western contemporary culture makes it hard to mentally consider ancient practices.

Furthermore, cultural differences will always exist.

The world is not *black & white*.

Even the summation that the entire Old Testament law is fulfilled in loving one another (Galatians 5:14), offers little clarity as a certain level of confusion still remains.

What

is

love?

Baby, don't hurt me.

I want to know what love is,

I want *you* to show me.

Think about it. Forget the context of those song lyrics, take 'em out, separate them from the whole and identify with me the potential for truth.

There is a scene in the movie "42" that shows a father and son attending a baseball game where Jackie Robinson is going to play. The boy is excited to be at the stadium attending a live Major League Baseball game. He probably had baseball cards of all his favorite players. In the 1960's, one ticket to a game would run you around $1.60. Take a second to dry your eye as you think about that.

As a child, the world seemed huge! I remember attending my first Chicago Cubs game in 1997. The stadium was enormous. Eventually, I grew up and became a season ticket holder, the stadium became another ball field to me, something I can easily get to and understand. The world seen through the eyes of an eleven-year-old boy at a Major League Baseball game is surreal. Dreams come alive.

Imagine that feeling. Then as the scene unfolds, many Caucasian patrons start yelling and heckling Jackie Robinson. They use the *N-word*. The boy looks confused. This was not baseball. This was not a dream. His world came crumbling down. Just as you begin to feel anger toward the adults and compassion for the boy, assuming the boy is probably wondering, "Why are they yelling at Jackie Robinson? He is a fantastic baseball player!" the boy musters up some courage and begins to yell the same things his father was yelling.

It broke my heart.

Often times, ignorance can be a terrible thing.

When it comes to thoughts and behaviors one is natural and one is learned. The boy in the movie represented the cycle of racism that was handed down from generation to generation. On that day, an evil thought was learned and *cultivated.*

By design, our bodies are self-preserving machines. When it aired, I would from time to time watch *1000 Ways to Die*. The premise was that it reenacted and scientifically explained weird and abnormal deaths that actually happened throughout all recorded history. One such death was someone freezing to death in a freezer. The person was discovered naked, as if they took off all of their clothes.

Long story short, the show explained how the body prioritizes parts of itself. When it gets too cold, circulation to the outer extremities is cut off. That is called, frostbite. The nervous system protects all major organs to keep the body alive. If relief and warmth does not arrive, the body will continue to cut off circulation allowing the blood to centralize in the center of the body and the brain. At that point, the body confuses itself and you believe you are getting too hot and are burning up. You react by shedding layers of clothes to cool off. Eventually, the body literally freezes as the heart gives out and no longer can pump any blood.

This leads me to believe that love goes beyond the physical. To effectively love someone or something, you have to put aside self-preservation.

Remember the pre-trip discussion in an airplane? If the oxygen masks drop, adults are to first put them on themselves and then the children?

Paradox.

One has to love others in order to love themselves. There are numerous studies that show that people who volunteer or regularly give of their time and resources without reciprocation are happier and healthier than those who do it less or not at all.[20]

I have heard it said that one must love themselves before they can love other people.

Here, love becomes a philosophy. Which one is correct, love others first, or myself first?

Love is not a philosophy.

Love is spiritual.

---

[20] http://www.health.harvard.edu/blog/volunteering-may-be-good-for-body-and-mind-201306266428

Jesus said in Matthew 5 that the law said *love your neighbor as yourself and hate your enemy.* Jesus went on to say that things were changing and that people were to love both neighbor *and* enemy. Consider your understanding and Western contemporary culture, this is a concept that plagues many people.

Jesus was emphasizing that love was not strictly physical and it was not strictly philosophical.

Physical: When a woman and a man make *love.*

Philosophical: What is love? Is it a *thing* or a *thought*?

Spiritual: Love is life and life is love.

What is our life force?

What drives you?

What is our purpose?

It has been determined that one of the biggest differences between animals and humans is the operating level of consciousness. Regarding love, animals, like humans, can positively engage in affection. Furthermore, some animals may even possess a certain level of attraction.

What animals cannot do is *die* for someone or something. Sure there are stories where animals die in the midst of saving a human, but it is widely accepted that the animal is unaware of the potential levels of danger. What they are aware of is that the person is in need and the animal must assist.

This animal may act instinctively or they could be acting out of affection as the person who they are attracted to is in danger, prompting the animal to intercede. The animal is not associating their action with *sacrifice.*

Real love means to sacrifice oneself for the sake of another. It is my desire to see every person experience the love of the Heavenly Father.

There is so much confusion in the church about the Father's pursuit of his creation. The Apostle Paul wrote in his second letter to the Corinthians that the ministry of the spirit was that of love. Whenever the oldness of the law is read, a veil falls over the faces of those who hear it. The veil blocks the individual from seeing the love of the Father. The only way one can see the Father is to look at him through Christ Jesus. The sacrifice of Jesus is love and so we look at the Father through the eyes of love.

When we understand the power of the Father's love we are set free. Free from the obligation to perfect ourselves and to instead look to the author and perfecter of one's faith, Christ Jesus. (Hebrews 12:2) The law is love. And in love, there is freedom.

Now the Lord is the Spirit, and where the Spirit of the Lord is, there is freedom.
2 Corinthians 3:17

Love sets us free.

The law points to our physical damnation.

Love points us to the Father, who is the Spirit.

Love does not bind us, it frees us.

May your spirit be free. Be free in the Father, for
the Father loves you.

Chapter 11:
Are You Allowed To Talk About Sex In A Christian Book?

I love a good story.

I have not met someone who does not appreciate a good story. From the most analytical paper-pushing accountant rehashing the details of their World of Warcraft victories over the weekend, to the hippie weed smoking coffee shop barista trying to determine exactly what did happen last weekend—not to say these are bad stereotypes, but one everlasting medium through which one person passes on accounts, true or false, truths or assumed truths, to another person happens most often through story.

Everyone has a story.

Even the worst of stories are still stories. Whether or not I care to hear about how you liked your hamburger because it tasted extra beefy and regardless of the lack of pretext for your story, it still meant something to you and you chose to include me in your tasty experience.

We will stop whatever it is we are doing to hear a good story, yeah?

Comedians make a living by telling funny stories.

Funerals are filled with funny and touching stories.

Politicians sling stories about their opponents.

My parents would break into pseudo-Chaucers stumbling through some incoherent poor excuse for a limerick whenever the topic of 'where do babies come from?' surfaced.

Evidently, whenever this question was raised, the dishwasher had to be loaded or the laundry had to be done. Had I figured out sooner those things got done quicker whenever I would ask *the* question, I could have worn my favorite jeans more often because they would have always been cleaned. I started to feel sorry for my parents. It is not an easy topic to discuss with children.

Sex.

What story do you tell to explain to them how mommy and daddy, every so often, do the horizontal shuffle to help make the world go round? It didn't matter, for I, the innocent oldest sibling explained with all humility and conviction—but mostly with condescending ill-intent, to my much younger sister that she was not in fact my biological sister, but the illegitimate love-child of a skunk and a porcupine. Not that this made any sense to her. Nonetheless, when she went crying to my parents about where she came from, well, without hesitation a household chore needed to be done. Unfortunately, that time it landed on me to do it.

Story is one of those things that really promote belonging.

With or without the intentioned purpose of the storyteller, a story brings into it all those involved and everyone who hears or reads it. We can't help it.

That is what makes great fiction.

I appreciate historical fiction. Take real people and put them in unreal situations.

Abraham Lincoln the vampire hunter.

Ben Franklin was a part of this secret society that kept hidden all the riches and jewels of the world.

Forest Gump helped inspire the logo for Joe Boxer.

Gandhi was a stuntman for James Dean.

I know Forest Gump is not a real person, but it is fun to think about 'untold' stories of prominent people.

It stretches the imagination.

It helps us let go of reason.

Some stories in the realm of fiction offer up to us a place where we truly can escape. It is not some high we endure as we watch and think afterward, "I wish my world was like that." People say these things, and they can because they don't know what their world would be like if they, in fact, experienced the fiction they just witnessed.

Some fiction can tragically remind me of the reality in which I am living.

The type of stories that I most appreciate let me return to my reality happy to have experienced something totally different with the affirmation that this is not anyone's reality.

Some fiction makes me pine after something that does not exist.

The same goes for non-fiction. We believe stories told by trusted sources. As children, whenever a teacher, preacher, politician, parent, or anyone in authority told us a story, we believed them.

That is the thing about stories, the more reliable the source, the more true it becomes. Much like the story about my parent's inability to have "the talk" with me. That story was a complete farce. I made it up.

To be honest, my dad did have a tough time wording 'the talk' with me.

As a fifth grader, the last thing on my mind was sex.

My interpersonal escapades with the opposite sex up until that time culminated in a few different scenarios: first it was the unwanted advance by me on a girl named Sara in Kindergarten. Dared, by "my friends," in an effort to "fit in" I kissed an unsuspecting Sara on the cheek. Believe it or not, but that Casanova move landed me in the corner. In first grade, I got down on one knee and exclaimed in front of the class my undying love and devotion to the principal's daughter. That is still one of my favorite stories from first grade.

That conversation about sex with my father at the age of twelve did offer me something I would never forget.

I did not understand it then, but I definitely understood it more as I got older. What my father did was not tell me some lame made up child's version of what happens when two people fall in love, kiss, and ten months later a baby comes out. Did I miss a step?

What he told me was a story of his life. This is what I love about stories. Stories do not have to necessarily make sense when we first hear them, but if there is one thing we can take away from the story, if one thing sticks, it gives way to truth.

Sometimes it is healthy to question our very existence as an individual and think back on our story. We wonder what could have been whether we had turned right instead of left.

What if I stayed with that person?

Where would I be had I, in its initial offering, bought stock in Apple computers?

Each route we could have taken certainly would have had a story worth telling, and most certainly would have been a story worth hearing. The problem that comes with this type of thinking is that in many cases, we begin to write the scripts to the "what if?" conversations we had over the years. When it compounds and interpolates into our lives these scripts begin, either to make us—with mortal blows—question our current situation, or cause us to escape into the realm of bad fiction or misleading non-fiction.

When we get lost in bad fiction, the consequences manifest themselves in combating identities—I am not talking about multiple personalities, I am talking about identity.

We become the person we are,

the person we thought we should be,

and ultimately, if we are maturing as people, asking the question,

"Am I becoming the person I could be?"

Hopefully, the person you are right now is not the person you were yesterday.

Physically, biologically, emotionally, cognitively, and even spiritually, each day is one day closer to the person you are becoming rather than the person you once were.

Whether or not, if given the chance or choice to go back in time and change some things about your life, entertaining the thought alone is living proof that there is something going on inside of you. For those of us honest enough to say we have at least one regret we would like to undo, we are also the same people who, in a healthy way, learn from that experience and apply those lessons to who we are in the ongoing formation of who we are becoming.

Those who say they have never had a regret are in denial. A passive aggressive nature works for a time, but slowly it eats away at the soul.

The inability to directly confront the hurdles in our lives makes for a long race.

All stories are stories of *belonging*.

When I think about all the people I have encountered and the people I have yet to experience, one truth jumps out at me.

No one is ever alone.

The narrative, in whatever situation I find myself, when I feel the world is on my shoulders and there is not another soul in sight is bad non-fiction. What happens in those stories is that when I, regardless of my emotional or spiritual location, am back to back with someone else, if I were to open my eyes and turn around I know there is someone-somewhere who is going through something similar.

If I were to, in faith, step into the darkness, toward the light, I will notice the markings and remnants of those who have been there before me.

Even when I intentionally seclude myself from the rest of the world, I am still included in the story of someone else.

There is no escaping it.

As long as I exist in the flesh walking around on this rotating rock, my story is intertwined somewhere.

I never want to be lost to the past for the past is a story of what was. My present falls on whether or not I turn the page and keep moving forward.

My story becomes part of a larger narrative.

My story, no matter how secluded, is always connected to someone else's story. Whether or not I like that truth, no matter how turned off I may become about the stories that surround me, the fact that I exist includes me in a narrative much larger than myself.

If I were to ask my father about those awkward moments in the basement of his Merrillville home, surrounded by white walls, me distracted by the water stain in the corner of one of the ceiling tiles, or the fact that I remember sitting on the floor staring up at my dad awaiting his sage advice; I doubt he would remember what he said. I do not remember the whole thing, but like any entertaining or boring story; there is usually one part that sticks in your mind.

"It gets harder. The older you get and the more you try to avoid it, the harder it becomes to not give in."

Sex needs a new story-teller.

This is a long introduction to sex, I get that. I sort of beat around the bush to get to this point and here I am, still avoiding the issue. In reality, I am not avoiding it, that is the whole purpose of this chapter.

Sex was something I saw in movies.

The stories I was told about sex involved all the negative things.

Sex is only for a man and wife who are married. Anything else and you submit yourself to the wrath of God.

Sex causes STD's. Seriously, I heard this at the school of redundancy school.

Girls can get pregnant from sex. This one does not affect me as much as I cannot get pregnant. Even then, if I was a round about seed planter, I do not think I would mind different versions of myself running around.

These are the top three. I will tackle the second two quickly.

Sex causes STD's. Nope. Sexually transmitted diseases describe the transfer of a bacteria/virus from one person to another. Sex cannot cause bacteria/virus to magically appear in one person and then transfer it to another. Even then, it is not a good enough reason to keep your pants on as people have an incredible amount of faith in condoms. Unfortunately, more young people can care less about this as cases of STD's/STI's are on the rise.[21]

Girls can get pregnant from sex. Well, duh. How else do more people get made? Scaring me with the unknown reality of parenting a child means little to me. However, if I had successfully fathered a child in the past and the experience had been wanting, then maybe, and I mean maybe this fact would make me think twice before petitioning a woman to remove her clothing. Another shot of tequila! Wait, I thought this was a Christian book.

Thirdly and certainly not least, *sex is only for a man and a wife.* I will gloss over the God's wrath part as I have witnessed countless people participate in full sexually active relationships without being married and God hath not smote them…yet. Insert vengeful laugh here.

Sex is a bothersome topic as any wise and mature person would suggest to a younger and immature person that sex really is a big deal. Not because of God per say, or moral obligation to some propagated idea surrounding sex, but because biologically, sex is a big deal.

There has to be a couple camps of people out there who promote some kind of healthy sexual encounters for all people of a consenting age. One of those is peddling sex as a normal biological function that has many benefits to one's well-being. I am not denying this is true, but there is a deeper *truth* to be discovered.

Why would some being, fictional or real, suggest to mankind (polygamy was commonplace in the Old Testament, but shunned in the New Testament) monogamy is the best option for a full life?

I find the biological implications to be somewhat significant. In unprotected sex, the way it has to be to have the best chance at making another human involves the scientific explanation of "exchanging bodily fluids." Part of the fluids exchanged in the nether regions during the deed includes blood.

Both partners.

Blood. (Covenant?)

---

[21] www.cdc.gov

Your DNA is given.

Passing each other on their way to the other person's body.

"Hello!"

With it, a bunch of other microscopic organisms.

Some organisms, which have the ability to plant, fertilize, and multiply.

This is one part in the physical side of sex.

This is the *making love* part.

The philosophical and equally biological part of love in relation to sex is what happens in the brain during climax.

Ew.

I just said climax.

Give me some props, I have managed to avoid saying penis and vagina.

Whoops.

You may be thinking, the brain is as much physical as the fluids passed between the bodies.

True, but it becomes philosophical and what I would suggest to be spiritual because of *what* happens in the brain.

As the deed continues between the two individuals, more often than not the man will climax before the woman. The point of climax or for the woman who does not reach climax, but may experience heightened arousal, the brain fires in a way that makes you *think* or *feel* you are literally connected to the other person.

It's science.

Tests show that for both men and women, the part of the brain that understands *acceptance* and *inclusion* goes crazy during states of heightened arousal.

The brain feels so connected that when the moment passes and the two separate in the awkward-getting-apart-from-each-other-dance, the chemicals and firings that insisted you were connected completely drop off and raise your cortisol and melatonin levels so much that you *feel* depressed or alone. Momentary clinical depression.

Crazy.

This is the problem with men and women who just met and allow their special places to meet and hang out for a few minutes.

Let's pretend for a second there is a spirit inside of you. That thing is going bonkers during a state of heightened arousal. It kind of explains why many people cry after sex. The forethought of sex is great in theory, but in regular practice with random individuals or a single individual without the security of them sticking around is traumatic to one's inner being.

I would submit that the biological functions both physical and spiritual were not accidental. It would be weird to suggest that in the random order of things, sex would cause the two involved to desire each other more *after* the action of procreation has been done.

The theory that all men just want to *spread their seed* implies on some level that men and women are animals and thus must act like animals.

Animals cannot show sacrificial love.[22] Humans can and so I submit to you for consideration that humans possess the ability to transcendently approach sex.

Reasonably, I suggest that sex is not as physical as many think. Perhaps sex is more spiritual in the sense that if we can track in the brain the processes associated with heightened arousal and the fact we can think about how sex impacts each individual emotionally; that sex is only physical in the exchanging of fluids,

---

[22] Jude verse 10

but it is spiritual in that it literally makes two separate entities *one,* if only for a moment.

The skeptic can say, "It's all *physical* you cannot prove that humans have a *spirit.*"

The best argument for spirit goes deep into the conversation concerning *consciousness*. What I am sure others have said, but I will echo here is a *level of self-awareness*. Take us a step further, but many people would say that a persons ability to speak sets them apart from every other living being on the planet. Not just communicate, but literally say words.

The ability to think about oneself is, ruling out any Holy Text's explanation, the best understanding we have for an indwelling *spirit*.

It is starting to get muddy, I am gonna get back to discussing sex.

Sex in the first century was an open act. Wedding celebrations lasted up to a week. After the ceremony, everyone would wait outside the room where the newlyweds went to consummate their marriage. In 2014, Middle Eastern culture is still open in many ways.

Even with all of the online social media, American culture is very privatized. Due to the privatization of some things, conversations about sex inside the Church have diminished. Moreover, all conversations pertaining to sex seem to have shifted to third party opinions by writers on websites, or a teenager talking to another teenager about sex.

Those who should be talking about sex, like grandparents and parents, aren't because it is *weird*.

I do not have a daughter, but the thought of fathering a daughter and then watching her grow up and eventually give herself to, what I hope will be, only one man gives me mixed emotions.

Sex is a good thing.

Everything that God created in the beginning was *good*. Just because sin entered the world does not mean that sex became *bad*.

Ephesians 5 talks about the mystery that is the similarities between God's relationship with the Church and a husband's relationship with his wife. This is not a chapter about marriage, but sex is an integral part of marriage (most successful marriages, anyway).

My emotions are mixed for a couple of different reasons, but focusing on the forethought of my daughter participating in that act with another person begs me to panic for a moment.

I believe that sex is *good,* so why would I panic about my daughter participating in something *good*?

It is probably because most people told me *bad things* about sex so that I would avoid it for as long as possible.

"It gets harder to avoid it."

The reality of sex is that if someone really wants it, they will go get it. The focus of our conversations about sex should not be about *avoiding* it, but rather about positioning someone for a proper perspective.

Sure I want my daughter to *avoid* sex, but not in the sense where she is thinking about and stressing out over whether or not it is a good decision to give up her flower to Tommy at the Junior High Sadie Hawkins Dance. If she avoids it then and avoids it all the way until she is married by then she has been conditioned to second-guess any type of physical intimacy due to the propagandizing of sex as evil and thus sees it as something that should be avoided.

I want my wife and I to set a solid example in appropriate and open conversation about the things that make sex,

good.

We believe in a God that created it.

Sex has a purpose.

The purpose of sex can be trivialized much like the questions, "Which came first, the chicken or the egg?"

Is the purpose of sex, pleasure or procreation, or both?

Is it for procreation and so to encourage procreation God made it pleasurable,

or did God create sex to manifest intimacy and remove barriers allowing for holistic acceptance by another person and by that process springs life…

Sex is grace.

The unadulterated experience of connectedness points to a fuller understanding of God. God longs for spiritual intimacy with his creation. This is why I deduce that sex is spiritual.

Sex is not about the act, it is about the experience.

God is not some incubus that fornicates with people in their sleep.

The experience of inclusion, acceptance, and oneness is the type of relationship that God offers on a daily basis.

God's grace makes that possible.

I wish sex had been explained to me in this way, as my understanding of sex now encourages me to save all that desire for intimacy or oneness with my wife. As I have the same desire for no barriers to be between me and my relationship with my wife, so I do not want there to be any barriers between myself and God.

My hope is that any single person who reads this hears from God as they pray about what I just submitted to them as a gracious way of discussing sex. That it does not matter how many people you have had sex with.

God's mercies are new everyday.

Re-examine your understanding of sex. Let your mind be renewed.

Sex is not about sex.

Sex is about grace.

Grace is about experience.

Save that experience for one person.

In between now and then, focus on the grace of God that beckons you to experience Him in all of His glory.

Parting Thoughts:

I asked myself a question at the end of the movie Maze Runner. *What was the point of everything I just experienced?*

How does this all fit together?

At the onset of this project, I wanted to discuss with relative brevity the issues that plagued my understanding of Christianity and the hurdles that hindered my experience of God.

Sure, there are a lot of other confusing issues in Christian Spirituality.

Prayer.

Worship.

Baptism.

Tithing.

God of the Old Testament versus God of the New Testament. IMMORTAL KOMBAT!

FIGHT! Spoiler alert, He is not as bi-polar as some people may think.

Fasting.

Church. Sunday mornings. Wednesday nights. Catholic stand-up, sit down, kneel, up, down, left hand in, left hand out. Baptist marathons. Charismatic or Pentecostal dance parties.

34,000 Christian denominations and growing. <— *That's nuts.*

Liturgies.

Sermons. Message. Word.

Prophecy.

Speaking in tongues. Other languages or the weird *tongues?*

Spiritual gifts.

Healing.
Immortality.

Ananias and Sapphira.

Communion also known as The Lord's Supper.

Angels and demons.

Modern day miracles.

The book of Revelation.

Christianese: Salvation, justification, sanctification, etc.

This project has become many things throughout the years. Sadly, it has taken me years to write it. Once I quit avoiding it, it only took months. Even reading it again and again, I ask myself *who is going to read this garbage?*

God told me not to worry about that, but to write it.

Writing this was a *process.* I have learned a lot in the past six years about process and *progress.* It has been a thrill learning from the Lord a heightened way of appraising the work that I do. See 2 Corinthians 3.

You made it this far and for that I am grateful. I hope in some way this has blessed you.

The point of all of this was to communicate the muddied waters of God & Christianity without getting long-winded or too preachy. I hope to have diverted your perspective for a moment and assisted in bringing clarity.

Part of the issue in the Church is that we all believe different things.

Jesus prayed, "May they all be one, as You, Father, are in Me and I am in You. May they also be one in Us, so the world may believe You sent Me." John 17:21

You may be thinking, *the Church is divided. Unity is impossible.*

I wrote about these areas in Christianity to offer up a basis for like-minded conversation. I wanted to avoid a, *Well this is what Nolan Recker thinks about this stuff* and "That's nice of him to share."

My prayer is that we, as a Church, pursue a unified understanding of the Good News that is evident in Scripture.

I am not saying I have obtained this unified truth and so bring it to you with great humility. On the contrary, the explanations I provided are where I am in my pilgrimage.

The blessing of life here on earth is beyond compare. Wherever we lay our head at night, all peoples have a reason to be thankful. It is a thankful heart that frees anyone to see clearly.

> "How happy are those who reside in Your house, who praise you continually. Happy are the people whose strength is in You, whose hearts are set on pilgrimage." Psalm 84:4-5

I did not put it in the block quote, but in your Bible between verses four and five is a word in italics, *Selah*.

It is worship without rules.

It is the "Amen!" that we yell out when the Spirit is moving in the sanctuary. There is so much soul we have to let the back door crack.

Again, thank you.

I am thankful for the opportunity and resources to even write this. I am thankful for the time spent with God in an effort to communicate what was laid on my heart. Don't freak out. This ain't Scripture or *new revelation*. However, some of the stuff I proposed to you in this book will be revelation to you. That, if you consider "renewing your mind," you may find Truth and in so doing "discern what is the good, pleasing, and perfect will of God." Romans 12:2

As Paul goes on to say there in Romans 12, I do not think this work is greater than what it is. This is a humble declaration of the things found in Scripture and what can be known plainly as made known by those in scholarly pursuit and those in prophetic ministry.

This work, I hope has been presented to you logically and sensibly, spurning you on to pursue *greater things*.

"As God has distributed a measure of faith to each one. Now as we have many parts in one body, and all the parts do not have the same function, in the same way we who are many are one body in Christ and individually members of one another." (verses 3-5)

As I quoted in the introduction, "For although we are walking in the flesh [according to what we can see], we do not wage war in a fleshly way, since the weapons of our warfare are not fleshly [tangible objects that can be held], but are powerful through God for the demolition of strongholds. We *demolish arguments* and every *high-minded* thing that is raised up against the *knowledge of God, taking every thought captive to the obedience of Christ* [reminding ourselves of Christ Jesus' obedience and not our obedience *to* Him]." 2 Corinthians 10:3-5

The Apostle John sums up the two commands that Jesus told everyone to follow in 1 John 3:23, "Now this is His command: that we believe in the name of His Son Jesus Christ, and love one another as He commanded us." The first command can be found in John 6:29 and the second command can be found in the same book, John 13:34.

This book fits together in the pulling down of strongholds in our belief systems. What we hold to be true in our hearts and minds must be questioned.

I first spoke of perspective.

Perspective matters.

What we believe about God matters.

Exchanging our thoughts in the pursuit of birthing a new mindset is imperative.

I hope by learning new information about the things discussed here will awaken in you a passion to seek out Truth!

Don't take my word for it.

Test every word that I have written.

Email me your questions at flybook2015@gmail.com

Question yourself.

Question me.

Question your pastor.

Most importantly, question God.

Seriously, it is O.K.

> "Therefore let us approach the throne of grace with boldness, so that we may receive mercy and find grace to help us at the proper time." Hebrews 4:16

What have you experienced because of time spent with God discussing the things presented here? Did you learn anything?

> "The one who is taught the message must share his goods with the teacher." Galatians 6:6

If so, what?

Tell the Lord!

> "Teach me Your way, Lord, and I will live by your truth. Give me an undivided mind to fear [understand the magnitude of] Your name. I will praise You with all of my heart…" (HCSB Psalms 86: 11-12)

If you are anything like me and have found yourself believing multiple things about God that all seem to contradict each other, then the verse above should definitely be your prayer. If there is nothing else that you take away from reading this book, seek the Lord in prayer reciting Psalm 86:11, "Give me an undivided mind [about You]."

Life is too short to wander around not giving a flying flip because there are *just too many opinions and you are unsure as to what is the right one.*

So, take this all for whatever you think it is worth.

Pursue the Lord for Truth.

May your prayer be for God to give you an undivided mind about His greatness. It may not all make sense,

but gaining clarity as to the importance of God and His grace?

Well, there are some who would trade all the riches of the world for that understanding.

The Good News for you and me?

Jesus already paid that.

So, take flight.

Go up.

Meet with God.

He's waiting.

About the Author:

Nolan and his wife, Emma along with their son Zeke William live in Bloomington, IL. As of the publishing of this book, Nolan serves as the primary teacher at Promise Land Ministries in Warrensburg, IL. Also, the Recker family is involved with a Vineyard Church campus getting planted in Bloomington/Normal.

This is Nolan's first published work. He intends to write more non-fiction and fiction works. He welcomes any and all feedback. He thoroughly enjoys face to face conversation while sipping on some coffee or a cold brew.

Drop him a note!

Find Nolan on Facebook.

He can also be reached at flybook2015@gmail.com